READY, STEADY . . . TEACH

P.E. Lesson Plans and Worksheets

Written by
LISA SPARKES, BSc.

First Published
January 05 in Great Britain by

PUBLISHING

© Lisa Sparkes 2005

The moral right of the author has been asserted in accordance with the
Copyright, Designs and Patents Act 1988

A CIP record for this work is available from the British Library

ISBN-10: 1-904904-12-2
ISBN-13: 978-1-904904-12-0

Typeset by Educational Printing Services Limited

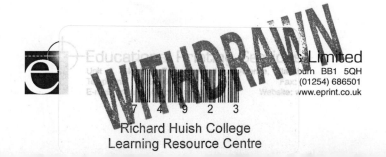

Educational . . . Limited
. . . urn BB1 5QH
. . . (01254) 686501
. . . www.eprint.co.uk

Acknowledgments —————

The author would like to thank her family and friends for all of their support and all at Northdown Primary School who encouraged her to write the book. A special thank you to Helen Marsh for both her guidance and motivation throughout writing the book.

Introduction

Physical Education (P.E.) in school is a very important area of education and health for children of all ages. PE can help children develop all areas of life skills including development of self esteem, confidence and values such as sportsmanship.

Areas of P.E. include activities such as dance, gymnastics and swimming. This book concentrates more on the area of games and sports. The aim of the book is to provide ideas of ways to break down skills of various sports, in a manner that suits age groups from Years 1 to 6, in a fun and memorable way.

The National Curriculum has a number of progression levels of ability on which children can be evaluated. These levels emphasise acquiring skills and developing them as well as selecting and applying the skills in the appropriate ways. With the aid of the activities and progression of each lesson plan structure, the children are able to carry out appropriate activities in order to achieve any level of the criteria.

Through using the guidance of the National Curriculum, previous knowledge of a degree in Sport, relevant courses and sport teachers, the plans have been developed and used and have proved overall to be successful in the development of the children's P.E. performances.

The key aim of the book is to give ideas which can then be developed or adapted by teachers/coaches, and are not necessarily the final plan for the sessions, but are a guide.

The majority of the skill areas covered in this book can provide a basic level of understanding for children to continue into Secondary school.

The worksheets for the lessons have been designed to provide activities for classes when P.E. may not be possible, due to circumstances such as bad weather.

They aim to provide details of the key rules, and understanding of sports through a visual and fun way of learning. Before the worksheets can be used to their full potential, it is vital that the group using them have been taught the rules, key factors, and have a basic understanding of people involved, positions and equipment used. The worksheets can then be used as either further learning or as part of evaluation of the children's learning of the theoretical area of P.E.

Contents

Chapter 1

Health and Safety

Before the beginning of every lesson a number of Health and Safety checks have to be carried out. Full Health and Safety checks can be recorded using an appropriate risk assessment form.

A basic list of checks would include:-

❑ The area in which the activity is taking place needs to be checked for any items that should not be there; such as broken glass or litter. Any items present should be removed and discarded in the correct way.

❑ The surface should be checked for any spillages. If outdoors, the conditions need to be checked to ensure they are suitable and safe; for example, if it has been raining.

❑ If equipment such as mobile football goals have been put together, they need to have been constructed properly, following the manufacturer's guidelines for use.

❑ Equipment needs to be regularly monitored to check for any damages that may have occurred, making it unsafe for use.

❑ Children who are participating, need to have removed any jewellery (including watches), hair that is longer than shoulder length must be tied back, and the correct footwear must be worn - this does not include school shoes.

❑ The children also need to be in practical clothing as some clothing can be restrictive.

❑ Any medical conditions that children have should be known before an activity commences, and any appropriate medication such as asthma pumps should be readily available.

Chapter 2

Warm Up Ideas

A variety of warm up games and stretches can be used when carrying out the lesson plans. Included in this chapter are a few examples of stretches and games to give an idea of what to use.

Stretches

General points to be remembered:

- A stretch should be held for 6-10 seconds.

- If the stretch hurts, then you are either trying too hard or are not stretching properly. If this is the case the coach should check the technique that is being used.

- Don't bounce when holding a stretch.

Games

- Animal Game

- Vehicle Game

- Car Game

- Number Game

- Beans

- Cups and Saucers

- High and Low Fives

Stretches

a. Neck - Side

Look over your right shoulder.

Feel the stretch down the left hand side of the neck.

Repeat stretch looking over the left shoulder.

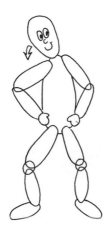

b. Neck - Side

Push the left ear to the left shoulder.

Feel the stretch down the right side of the neck.

Repeat pushing the right ear to the right shoulder.

c. Neck - Front and back

Look up to the ceiling.

Feel the stretch under the chin.

Push chin to chest and feel the stretch at the back of the neck.

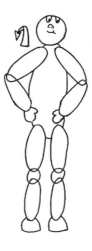

d. Arms - Top and shoulder

Hold the right arm out to the side, away from the body.

Bring the arm across the front of the body.

Hold the arm with the left hand, and pull into the chest.

Feel the stretch along the outside of the arm.

Repeat with the left arm across the body.

e. Arms - Under the arms

Hold the right arm above your head.

Bend at the elbow and place your hand on your back.

Hold your elbow with your left hand.

Feel the stretch underneath the arm, (Triceps).

Repeat using the left arm.

f. Legs - Lower leg (Calf)

Stand with feet shoulder width apart.

Feet face the same way in front of you.

Step the left leg forwards.

Bend the front leg (left), keep the back leg straight and
both feet should remain flat on the floor.

Feel the stretch in the back of the right leg, especially
the lower part (calf muscle).

Now repeat stepping the right leg forward.

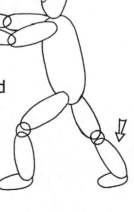

g. Legs - Inside (Groin)

Stand with feet shoulder width apart.

Feet facing forwards.

Step the right leg out to the side.

Keep feet in line and facing forwards.

Bend right leg and keep the left one straight.

Feel the stretch on the inside of the legs.

Return to standing position and repeat stepping the left leg.

h. Leg - Top of the thigh (Quadriceps)

Stand with feet shoulder width apart.

Slightly bend the left leg and pull the right foot up behind you holding the foot with the right hand, and pull towards the bottom.

If the stretch is felt within the knee area, relax the pull and don't bend the right leg so much.

The stretch should be felt in the thigh. Now reverse.

For extra balance hold the opposite ear with the hand that is free.

i. Legs - Back of the thigh (Hamstrings)

Stand with feet shoulder width apart.

Step the left leg forward.

Bend the back leg (right), keep the front leg straight.

Both feet should remain flat on the floor.

Feel the stretch in the back of the left leg.

Use hands for support and lean on the bent leg.

Now repeat stepping the right leg forward.

Games

a. Animal Game

The children run around in spaces, and when an animal is called the children have to imitate that animal. Encourage the children not only to make the sound of the animal but to use the whole of their bodies to be as much like that animal as possible.

For example, if a chicken is called they can use their legs, arms, neck and facial expressions to imitate a chicken.

Preferable age groups: Years 1 and 2.

b. Vehicle Game

The children run in a variety of spaces, and when a vehicle type is called children use all of their body to move like that vehicle.

For example: Train, car, plane etc.

Preferable age groups: Years 1 and 2.

c. Car Game

Jog and listen to instructions that are called. Before the exercise, explain each instruction.

Gear 1: Walk
Gear 2: Fast walk
Gear 3: Jog
Reverse: Walking backwards

Preferable age groups: Years 1 to 4.

d. Number Game

This game can have many variations.

The children can either run around in lots of different spaces, or follow a leader.

Using numbers to associate an action, the children are firstly told what each number represents, for example:

      1 = jump
      2 = touch the floor
      3 = skip etc.

The children then run and when a number is called they carry out the action.

Preferable age groups: Years 1 to 6.

e. Beans

The children have to carry out the action that each bean represents. At the start of the game, introduce what action each bean has.

For example:
      jumping bean is jumping on the spot
      runner bean is running.

The children then listen for what bean is called and carry out that movement. Variations can be used, using any bean and action.

For older groups, if those children who don't carry out the action correctly sit out, they can become judges and the last one in the game, wins.

Preferable age groups: Years 1 to 6.

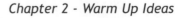

f. Cups and Saucers

Preparation
Place an equal number of marker cones facing
up and down (as illustrated).
Divide the group into two teams.
One group aims to get cones facing up.
One group aims to get the cones facing down.

Key
◣ = Cones Up
◡ = Cones down

Variations depending on group
- Both teams go and turn the cones at once, emphasise to be careful of others.
- Tag team, one person goes into the middle and turns a cone, tags the next person to go and joins the back of the line and so on.

Preferable age groups: Years 3 to 6.

g. High and Low Fives

This game helps to stretch both sides of the body as well as increasing awareness of others and of space.

Children run around in a given area. As they pass each other they hold out either of their hands at either head or waist height, palms facing down.

The aim is to gently touch the approaching person on their hand. The children look for others' hands to touch and at the same time extend their arm to be touched. Children are encouraged to use both hands and both high and low movements.

Remind the children they are not trying to slap each other but to just gently touch the other children's hands.

Preferable age group: Years 3 to 6.

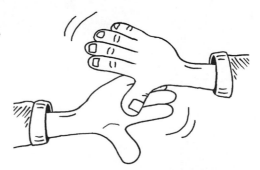

Chapter 3

Lesson Plans

Introduction

The layout for the lesson plans for all age groups focuses on basic skills; Ball Skills, Football, Running, and Kwik Cricket. These sports cover individual, team and striking games.

The skills from each sport are broken down, and then gradually as each lesson progresses, all the skills, team play and rules of a complete game or relevant activity are combined.

For Years 1 and 2, lessons focus on the basic skills of hand eye co-ordination in ball skills, and the basic skills of football to develop co-ordination using other areas of the body.

For Years 3 to 6, lessons aim to develop understanding by using examples from an individual, team or striking sport. The lessons are all at a basic level with the flexibility to adapt the difficulty level to suit those children more or less able, therefore involving children of all Primary age and ability.

Part 1

Years 1 and 2

A - Ball Skills

Week 1: Basics of ball control and co-ordination

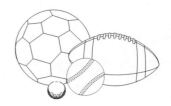

Warm up: Animal Game.

Main activity:
Divide the class into pairs and stand them opposite each other. Each pair needs a ball and should be separated by cones.

Activity 1: Pass and Roll

Ask the children to roll the ball to each other making sure they bend their knees when rolling and receiving the ball.

When they roll the ball, it is important to make sure that the children swing their arms, through their legs, whilst holding the ball with both hands, and then roll it.

Some children may put the ball on the ground and then push it. Try to encourage the children not to use this technique.

Activity 2: Throw and Catch

The children throw the ball to their partners using both hands. When their partner catches the ball, explain to the children that catching the ball is like 'hugging' a teddy. The 'hug' technique should help the children to draw the ball into their body, producing a better catching technique instead of pushing the ball away.

Cool down/Summary:
Basic gentle stretches with the group. If the group is positioned into a circle they can then interact and discuss what the main coaching points of the lesson are whilst doing a cool down.

Variations:
For both of these activities varying the size of the ball will help the children learn these skills in a variety of ways, and is very good for developing their hand/eye co-ordination.

Topic: Ball Skills

Week: 1

Year Group: 1-2

Objectives/Learning Outcomes:
To learn the basic throws and how to catch.

Special Requirements: Correct footwear and clothes.

Duration: 30 minutes.

Duration: (Minutes)	Activity	Coaching Points	Organisation	Resources/ Equipment
5	Animal Game	Use all the parts of the body as much as possible.	As a class in an open space	Whistle
20	Pass and Roll Throw and Catch	Bend knees to roll and receive. Swing arms. Don't push the ball. Use both hands. 'Hug' to catch.	In pairs	Cones Balls of various sizes Whistle
5	Stretch	Can the group remember coaching points?	As a class	N/A

Layout of Activity

Start with the distance between the cones fairly small, and gradually increase it as the children become more confident and can perform the task with ease.

 = Cone layout

Chapter 3 - Lesson Plans: Part 1 - Years 1 and 2

Week 2: Introducing different throws, abbreviated as 'S.C.R.U.B.'

Warm up: Vehicle Game.

Main activity:
Children are placed in pairs and stand opposite each other with a netball between them.

Activity 1: 'S' is for Shoulder Pass

The aim is to throw the ball from shoulder level, using one hand. Hold the ball with one hand and bend the throwing arm, as you extend the arm push the ball upwards and forwards towards your partner.

Activity 2: 'C' is for Chest Pass

When throwing the ball from a chest pass, firstly hold your thumbs together and form a 'W' shape with your hands. This is the position your hands are in when holding the ball.

Pushing the elbows in to the side and with your hands at chest height, push the ball from under the chin, aiming to throw the ball in a straight line towards your partner.

Activity 3: 'R' is for Rolling

As the previous week, ask the children to roll the ball to each other making sure they bend their knees when rolling and receiving the ball.

When they roll the ball, it is important to make sure that the children swing their arms, holding the ball between their legs with both hands and then roll it.

Some children may put the ball on the ground and then push it, try to encourage the children not to use this technique.

Activity 4: 'U' is for Underarm

Hold the ball with both hands and throw the ball upwards and forwards to their partners.

Activity 5: 'B' is for Bounce Pass

Hold the ball as you would hold it for a chest pass, remembering just under the chin and elbows in. This time as you extend the arms the aim is to push the ball forwards and downwards aiming for the middle of you and your partner.

Cool down/Summary:
Ask the group to stand in a circle and the coach/teacher stands in the middle with the ball. The aim is for the person who receives the ball to return it to the person in the middle exactly as it was thrown to them. This gives the other children in the group a chance to be stretching whilst they wait for their turn and to watch how it should be done. If there are any mistakes, can the children tell you what they are? It is also a good way to analyse what the children have learnt.

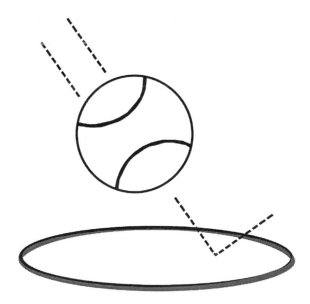

Variations:
Using most of these throws involves both hands, however, once the technique has been mastered using both hands and a netball, the techniques can be changed for using a smaller ball and eventually one hand.

Shoulder Pass
With a small ball, practise throwing with one hand, over arm.

Chest Pass
With a small ball, throw one handed to your partner.

Roll
With a small ball and using one hand, bend and roll the ball from the side which you are rolling from, as in bowling.

Underarm
The same technique with one hand and a smaller ball.

Bounce Pass
With a small ball, one handed bounce to your partner.

Group Game
This game will help the children observe the correct technique of a throw and to then copy.

Ask the children to stand in a circle. Stand in the centre of the circle and throw the ball. Instruct the children to watch the way you throw. They must then return the ball to you in the same way. The correct technique must be used from the head, right down to the feet.

Get the other children to observe if the ball was sent in the right way, and to spot what is not done correctly. If they do not notice the mistake, explain what was wrong and demonstrate the correct technique.

Topic: Ball Skills

Week: 2

Year Group: 1-2

Objectives/Learning Outcomes:
To learn various throws. Abbreviated as 'S.C.R.U.B.'

Special Requirements: Correct footwear and clothes.

Duration: 30 minutes.

Duration: (Minutes)	Activity	Coaching Points	Organisation	Resources/ Equipment
5	Vehicle Game	Use all of the body to move.	As a class in an open space	Whistle
15/20	Shoulder Pass Chest Pass Rolling Under Arm Bounce Pass	Push from shoulder. Push from chest. Swing arms. Both hands. Chest pass downwards.	Class into pairs. 1 ball between a pair. Use cones for correct distance apart.	Cones Netball balls Whistle
5/10	Group Game	Return the ball to the person in the middle copying exactly what they did.	Group stand in a circle, teacher/coach in the middle.	Ball

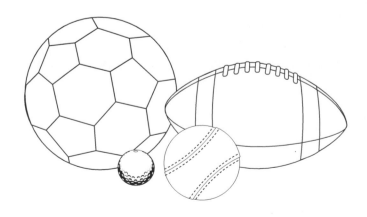

Main Activity Layout

Start with the distance between the cones fairly small, and gradually increase it as the children become more confident and can perform the task with ease.

GROUP GAME:

Group stand in a circle, teacher/coach stands in the centre.

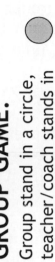

= Cone layout

Week 3: Introducing targets

Warm up: Number Game.

Main activity:
Put the class into two groups, to work in a small circuit and explain what a target is.

Activity 1: Rolling

In their groups, the children take it in turns to roll the ball and aim it so that the ball goes in between two cones. Recap the main coaching points from Week 1 about rolling techniques.

Activity 2: Bounce Pass

Using the previous knowledge of a bounce pass with a netball, the aim is to bounce the ball in the hoop that is in the middle of the pair, and for it to reach their partner.

Cool down/Summary:
Get the children to walk, jog, skip or jump in all different spaces when given the command to do so. Stretch and recap the main coaching points so far.

Variations:
The distance which the children stand from the targets can be adjusted to either increase or decrease the difficulty level of the task.

The size of the targets can also be adjusted to suit difficulty levels.

As before, the size of the ball can also be varied accordingly, to either increase or decrease the difficulty of the task.

Topic: Ball Skills

Week: 3

Year Group: 1-2

Objectives/Learning Outcomes:
Introducing targets.

Special Requirements: Correct footwear and clothes.

Duration: 30 minutes.

Duration: (Minutes)	Activity	Coaching Points	Organisation	Resources/ Equipment
5	Number Game	Run in all directions.	As a class in an open space	Whistle
20	Rolling Bounce Pass	Introduce a target. Recap correct techniques for throws.	Class is divided into 2 groups over the two activities and swap.	Cones Balls of various sizes Hoops
5	Gentle jog	Discuss how using targets changes the activity.	As a class	N/A

Activities Layout

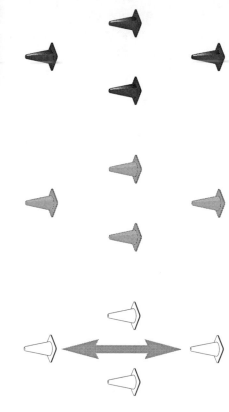

Activity 1: Rolling

Aim to roll the ball through the cones and to your partner opposite.

Activity 2: Bounce Pass

Aim to bounce the ball in the hoop and to your partner opposite.

 = Hoop

 = Cone

Chapter 3 - Lesson Plans: Part 1 - Years 1 and 2

Week 4: Advanced targets

Warm up: Number Game.

Main activity:
The aim of this week's lesson is to recap Week 3's activities with the original distances and targets and slowly develop the difficulty level according to how the children manage with them.

If working in small groups and on a circuit, the stations can vary their distances between the throw/rolling point to the target and also vary the size of the targets that are used.

The other stations can then have a standard distance from the targets but vary the size of the targets.

If some children have mastered the distance and can perform the task with ease, then they can try with a smaller ball and eventually one hand.

Cool down/Summary:
Get the group to stand in a circle and the coach/teacher stands in the middle with the ball. The aim is for the person who receives the ball to return it to the person in the middle exactly as it was thrown to them. This gives the other children in the group a chance to watch how it should be done or, if there are any mistakes, can the children tell you what they are? It is also a good way to analyse what the children have learnt and if any improvement has happened since Week 2.

Topic: Ball Skills

Week: 4

Year Group: 1-2

Objectives/Learning Outcomes:
Advanced targets.

Special Requirements: Correct footwear and clothes.

Duration: 30 minutes.

Duration: (Minutes)	Activity	Coaching Points	Organisation	Resources/ Equipment
5	Number Game	Follow instructions	As a class in an open space	Whistle
20	Rolling Bounce Pass	Recap correct techniques. Explain about shorter the distance, softer the throw. Further the distance, harder the throw.	Class is divided into 2 groups over the two activities and swap.	Cones Balls of various sizes Hoops
5	Group Game	Return the ball to the person in the middle copying exactly what they did.	Group stand in a circle, teacher/coach in the middle.	Ball

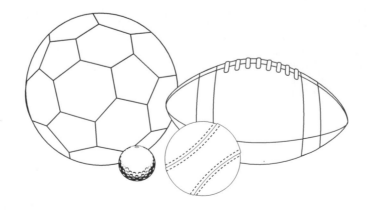

Activities Layout

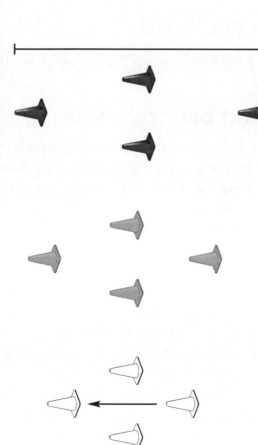

Activity 1: Rolling

Gradually increase the distance from the cones and the targets.

Activity 2: Bounce Pass

Gradually increase the distance from the cones and the targets.

 = Cone

◯ = Hoop

Week 5: 'S.C.R.U.B.' and targets in a circuit

Warm up: Car Game.

Main activity:
Demonstrate firstly what is required at each station. Divide the class into small groups and put one group on each station. If possible, record who the groups are and what stations they complete. Those they did not complete can be worked on the following week.

Activity 1: Rolling a small ball through a small target

Recap coaching point previously used in Week 4.

Activity 2: Throwing at various targets

Similar to netball practice, aim a netball at the target wall, or a series of targets at different heights, or distances. What are the best throws to use on certain targets?

Activity 3: Underarm throwing

In pairs, practise underarm throwing. Depending upon the children's ability, choose a variety of balls.

Activity 4: Bouncing with one hand

Introducing a basketball, each child practises bouncing the ball with both hands, left then right.

Activity 5: Chest passes and bounce passes

In groups of four they each stand on a corner of a square, which has a hoop in the middle. If they decide to pass it to the person diagonal to them, they use a bounce pass, to bounce the ball into the hoop to their intended person. If they decide to pass the ball to the left or right of them, they use a straight chest pass.

Cool down/Summary:
Instruct the children to jog around in a given area avoiding any equipment and each other. When an instruction is given the children should then carry it out. For example, if 'Girls and blue cones' is called, all the girls walk (or whatever move has been stated) to a blue cone and return it to a place that they have been told to put it.

To minimise any bumps you can state that they must walk around in spaces, and perhaps when calling the instruction you can limit it to certain people for example, people with blue eyes etc. Make sure that everyone gets a turn. This is also a great way to get the children to pack the equipment away at the end of a session.

Chapter 3 - Lesson Plans: Part 1 - Years 1 and 2

Week 6: To complete the circuit from Week 5

Warm up: High and Low Fives.

Main activity:
To start the session, arrange the children into pairs, and give one ball to each pair.

Can the children remember the five throws for 'S.C.R.U.B.'? Recap what they are and then practise them.

Briefly recap and see what the children can remember about what each station involves. If possible put the children in the same groups as before and start them on an activity they may not have had time to do the previous week.

The children then continue to practise each station, working on improving their skills if repeating an activity.

Cool down/Summary:
A repeat of Week 5. Instruct the children to jog around in spaces avoiding any equipment and each other. When an instruction is given the children should then carry it out. For example, if 'Girls and blue cones' is called, all the girls walk (or whatever move has been stated) to a blue cone and return it to a place that they have been told to put it.

To minimise any bumps you can state that they must walk around in spaces, and perhaps when calling the instruction you can limit it to certain people; for example, people with blue eyes etc. Make sure that everyone gets a turn. This is also a great way for the equipment to be packed away at the end of a session.

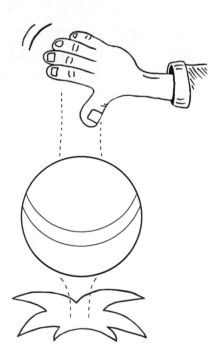

Week 7: Advanced 'S.C.R.U.B.' circuit

Warm up: Animal Game.

Main activity:
Children have now had two weeks to familiarise themselves with the 'S.C.R.U.B.' throws and the circuit, and this week can vary according to how well the children have progressed.

If the children are having difficulty, then this week can be used to spend more time trying to develop the skills and spend longer on each station.

However, if children are generally progressing well on each activity, this week the circuit can be set out with increased difficulty levels. Again using distance from targets, size of targets and different sized balls. (Refer to page 27.)

Cool down/Summary:
A repeat of Week 5. Instruct the children to jog around in spaces avoiding any equipment and each other. When an instruction is given the children should then carry it out. For example, if 'Girls and blue cones' is called, all the girls walk (or whatever move has been stated) to a blue cone and return it to a place that they have been told to put it.

To minimise any bumps you can state that they must walk around in spaces, and perhaps when calling the instruction you can limit it to certain people; for example, people with blue eyes etc. Make sure that everyone gets a turn. This is also a great way for the equipment to be packed away at the end of a session.

Topic: Ball Skills

Week: 5-7

Year Group: 1-2

Objectives/Learning Outcomes:
A circuit with 'S.C.R.U.B.' and targets.

Special Requirements: Correct footwear and clothes.

Duration: 30 minutes.

Duration: (Minutes)	Activity	Coaching Points	Organisation	Resources/ Equipment
5	Car Game Animal Game High/Low Fives	Remember instructions.	As a class in an open space	Whistle
20	'S.C.R.U.B.' Circuit	Remember correct techniques. Demonstrate each activity.	In small groups move around the circuit when instructed to.	Cones Basketballs Netballs Hoops Various sized balls.
5	Discussion	Can the children identify the main points of each station?	As a class	N/A

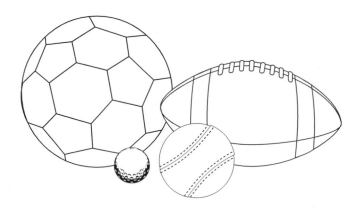

Activity 1: Rolling through a target

Activity 2:
Underarm Passing

Activity 3:
Various Targets

If available use a target wall to experiment which throws are better suited for various target sizes and heights. If there is no target wall, set out targets and various distances.

Activity 4: Chest Passes and Bounce Passes

Activity 5:
Bouncing with one hand

Practising various bouncing with a basketball.

To pass left and right use Chest Pass.
To pass diagonally use Bounce Pass into hoop.

△ = Cone   ○ = Hoop   ● = Basketball   ◈ = Target

Chapter 3 - Lesson Plans: Part 1 - Years 1 and 2

Ball Skills - Summary

What types of throw have the children learnt?

S.C.R.U.B.
Shoulder
Chest
Roll
Underarm
Bounce

When catching the ball what do you do with it?

Hug the ball.

What are the main points to remember for each throw?

Shoulder Pass
Push the ball from shoulder height.
Push the ball upwards.

Chest Pass
Two hands behind the ball.
Elbows in to the side.
Push the ball in a straight line forward.

Rolling
Bend your knees when rolling and receiving.
Swing the arms.

Underarm
Use both hands.

Bounce Pass
Push from your chest.
Use both hands.

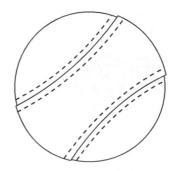

B - Football

Week 1: Basic ball control

Warm up: Number Game.

Main activity:
The class is divided into two groups over two activities and then half way through, they swap.

Activity 1: Passing

In pairs, the children pass the ball to each other using the side of their foot.

Before they start the activity, ask the children to touch the inside of their feet using their hands. This will make them aware of what part of the foot they need to kick with.

Their non-kicking foot is placed next to the ball and points to where they want the ball to go, which in this case is their partner. Explain the kicking motion acts a bit like a golf club hitting a golf ball, in regards to the swing of the leg to get power behind the pass.

When receiving the ball, emphasise stopping the ball with the side of the foot first, before passing it back in order to gain better control of the ball.

The children then practise this using both legs.

Activity 2: Dribbling

The aim of this is to encourage ball control using dribbling skills in and out of cones, using both feet and this time using all areas of the foot.

Explain to the children that the part of the body mentioned in the sport is the foot, not the hands, as some children may be tempted to use their hands if they lose control of the ball.

Briefly explain that the only person who can always use their hands is the goal keeper, and players that take throw-ins.

Cool down/Summary:
Basic gentle stretches with the group. If the group is positioned into a circle they can then interact and discuss what the main coaching points were of the lesson whilst doing a cool down.

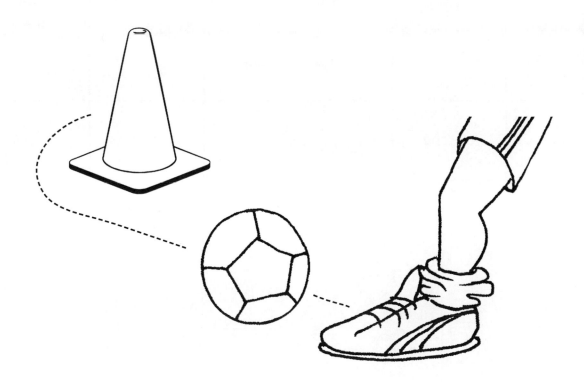

Topic: Football

Week: 1

Year Group: 1-2

Objectives/Learning Outcomes:
The breakdown of football skills.

Special Requirements: Correct footwear and clothes.

Duration: 40 minutes.

Duration: (Minutes)	Activity	Coaching Points	Organisation	Resources/ Equipment
5-10	Number Game	Remember instructions	As a class in an open space	N/A
20-30	Passes Dribbling	- Inside of foot - Look up - Use both feet	In pairs	Cones Whistle Footballs
5	Stretches	Recap main points	As a class	N/A

Activity Layout

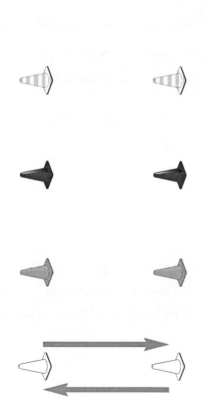

Dribbling

Dribble ball around cones:

- Right Foot,
- Left Foot,
- Both,
- Use all parts of both feet.

Passing

- Use side of the foot.
- Stop the ball before passing back.
- Those that find this too easy, stop the ball to the side and pass back. (Coach to demonstrate.)
- Non kicking foot next to the ball, and face the way you want to kick.

 = Cone

Week 2: Skills circuit

Warm up: High and Low Fives

Main activity:
Divide the class into three groups and recap the techniques for dribbling and passing.

Activity 1: Dribbling around cones

The aim of this is to encourage ball control using dribbling skills in and out of cones, using both feet and this time using all areas of the foot.
Explain to the children that the part of the body mentioned in the sport is the foot, not the hand, as some children may be tempted to use their hands if they lose control of the ball.

Activity 2: Pass and Stop

Using the same technique as in Week 1 (refer to page 36) the children practise passing to each other in pairs. Remembering to stop the ball before returning it.

Activity 3: Dribble and Shoot

The aim of the task is to dribble the ball around the cones as in station 1, but not to dribble back, instead stop the ball with their feet and take a shot at goal.
Explain that when they shoot they should keep the same techniques as passing except the target is now a goal and not their partners. So in order to see where they are aiming the ball, they need to stop the ball, and look up at the target before shooting.

Cool down/Summary:
A repeat of Week 1: Basic gentle stretches with the group. If the group is positioned into a circle they can then interact and discuss what the main coaching points were of the lesson whilst doing a cool down.

Topic: Football

Week: 2

Year Group: 1-2

Objectives/Learning Outcomes:
Skills circuit.

Special Requirements: Correct footwear and clothes.

Duration: 30 minutes.

Duration: (Minutes)	Activity	Coaching Points	Organisation	Resources/ Equipment
5-10	High and Low Fives	Encourage emphasis on high and low.	As a class	Whistle
20-30	Skills Circuit: - Dribbling - Passing - Dribble and Shoot	Recap correct techniques. Demonstrate each activity from Week 1.	Small groups. Will rotate each activity when instructed.	Cones Whistle Footballs
5	Stretches	Discuss and continue next.	As a class	N/A

Activity Layout

Passing

- Use side of the foot.
- Stop the ball before passing back.
- Those that find this too easy, stop the ball to the side and pass back (Coach to demonstrate).
- Non kicking foot next to the ball, and face the way you want to kick.

Dribbling

Dribble ball around cones:
- Right Foot,
- Left Foot,
- Both,
- Use all parts of both feet.

Dribble and Shoot

- Use both feet to dribble.
- Stop the ball on the last cone.
- Look up and take a shot.
- Collect ball and return to line.

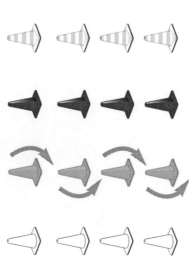

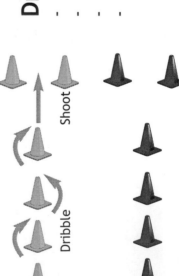

Shoot

Dribble

▷ = Cone

Week 3 and 4: Combining basic skills

Warm up: Number Game.

Main activity:
Divide the children into three groups as equally as possible over each activity.

Activity 1: Dribble and Shoot

The aim of this is to encourage ball control using dribbling skills in and out of cones, using both feet and this time using all areas of the foot. Explain to the children that the part of the body mentioned in the sport is the foot, not the hand, as some children may be tempted to use their hands if they lose control of the ball.

Activity 2: Dribble and Pass

As with the dribbling around the cones, using all areas of both feet, this time when they reach the end to come back, they stop the ball and control it ready to pass the ball back to the next person whose go it is in the line. Once they have passed the ball back they jog/walk back to the end of the line.

Activity 3: Pass in small groups

The children have practised passing in pairs and now the introduction of small groups starts the development to teamwork. As well as recapping passing techniques it is important to explain the importance of everyone in the group working together so that they all have a turn.
Children on this activity stand in a square and practise their passes, always stopping the ball before they pass to someone else.

Cool down/Summary:
Instruct the children to jog around in spaces avoiding any equipment and each other. When an instruction is given the children should then carry it out. For example, if 'Girls and blue cones' is called, all the girls walk (or whatever move has been stated) to a blue cone and return it to a place that they have been told to put it. To minimise any bumps, you can state that they must walk around in spaces, and perhaps when calling the instruction you can limit it to certain people; for example, people with blue eyes etc. Make sure that everyone gets a turn. This is also a great way for the equipment to be packed away at the end of a session.

Topic: Football

Week: 3 and 4

Year Group: 1-2

Objectives/Learning Outcomes:
Skills circuit.

Special Requirements: Correct footwear and clothes.

Duration: 30 minutes.

Duration: (Minutes)	Activity	Coaching Points	Organisation	Resources/ Equipment
5-10	Number Game	Follow instructions	As a class in an open space	Whistle
20-30	Dribble and Pass Dribble and Shoot Passing in groups	Describe each activity. Techniques exactly the same as when carried out individually.	In groups divided over each activity.	Cones Whistle Footballs
5	Stretches	Recap performances	As a class	N/A

Activity Layout

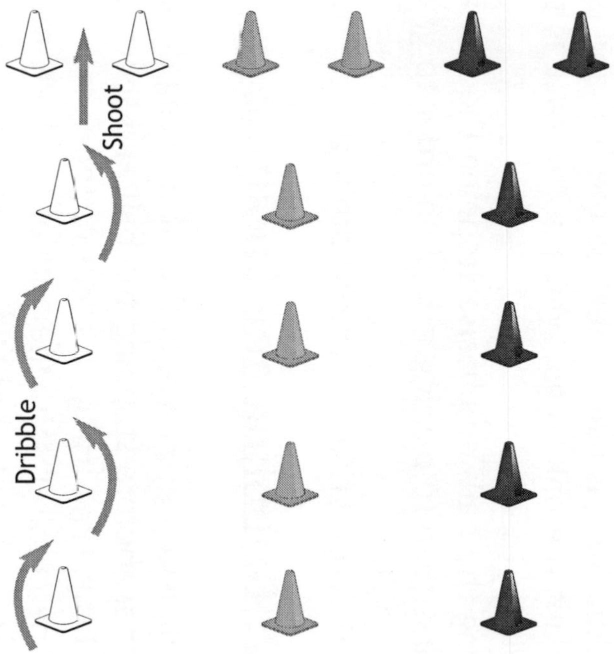

Passing in groups

Pass

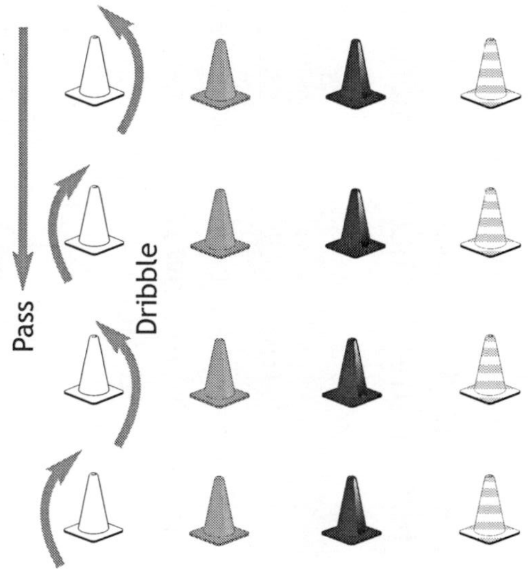

Dribble and Shoot

Shoot

Dribble

Dribble and Pass

Dribble

Pass

△ = Cone

Week 5: Combining basic skills with targets

As Week 1 but this time encourage the children to be aware that they have targets they are aiming to get the ball between.

Warm up: Number Game.

Main activity:
The class is divided into two groups over two activities and then half way through, they swap.

Activity 1: Passing

In pairs, the children pass the ball through the target to each other using the side of their foot.
Their non-kicking foot is placed next to the ball and points to where they want the ball to go, which in this case is through the target to their partner.
When receiving the ball, emphasise stopping the ball with the side of the foot first, before passing it back in order to gain better control of the ball.
The children then practise this using both legs.

Activity 2: Dribbling and Shooting

The aim of this is to encourage ball control using dribbling skills in and out of cones, before stopping the ball and shooting, using both feet and this time using all areas of the foot.
Point out to the children that the part of the body mentioned in the sport is the foot, not the hand, as some children may be tempted to use their hands if they lose control of the ball.

When shooting from various distances, different power will be needed in the shot. Explain that the shorter the distance, the less power needed and the further the distance the more power needed.

Cool down/Summary:
Follow my leader, encourage the leader to do exercises that are suitable for cool down, for example slower movements and stretches. This will help the children to work together and watch and follow instructions.

Topic: Football

Week: 5

Year Group: 1-2

Objectives/Learning Outcomes:
Using the basic skills and targets.

Special Requirements: Correct footwear and clothes.

Duration: 30 minutes.

Duration: (Minutes)	Activity	Coaching Points	Organisation	Resources/ Equipment
5-10	Number Game	Follow instructions	As a class in an open space	Whistle
20-30	Pass through target Dribble and shoot	Recap techniques for each activity. Shorter the distance, softer the pass. Accuracy not power for smaller targets.	Small groups	Cones Whistle Footballs
5	Stretches	Explain distance and accuracy.	As a class	N/A

Activity Layout

Activity 2: Dribble and Shoot

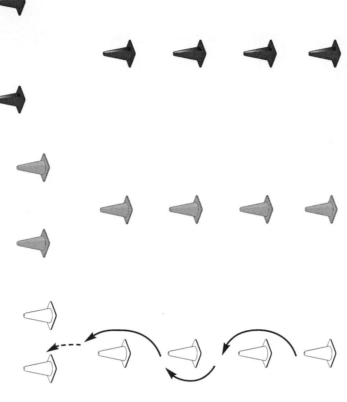

- Use both feet to dribble.
- Stop the ball on the last cone.
- Look up and take a shot.
- Collect ball and return to line.
- Distance from where you shoot from and the size of the goal can vary to decrease or increase difficulty level.

△ = Cone

Activity 1: Pass through targets

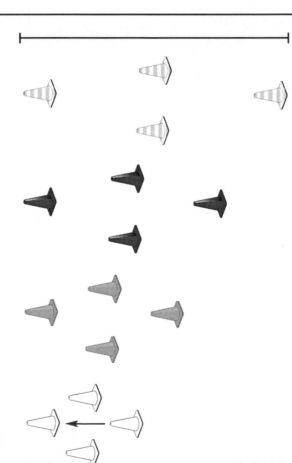

- Use previous passing techniques.
- Targets can vary in size to decrease or increase the difficulty.
- The distance from the targets can also decrease or increase to vary the difficulty.

Weeks 6 and 7: Team matches

As Week 1 but this time encourage the children to be aware that they have targets they are aiming to get the ball between.

Warm up: Cups and Saucers Game.

Main activity:
In Week 6 divide the class into four teams, and two matches will be played along side each other.

Explain to the children the parameters of each pitch and which teams they are playing against. At this level explain that all those wearing the same colour bibs are a team and that the aim is for everyone to kick the ball. Also explain which goal each team are aiming to score in.

In Week 7 the principle is the same except the class are just divided into two teams and one big match is played.

Use the observation of the matches to see if any of the previous skills are demonstrated by anyone. From these observations, what needs to be worked on and developed can be identified for future reference in coaching the football lessons.

Cool down/Summary:
Continuing an introduction of team work, children are put into teams in lines one behind the other. Making sure that the person in front is about arms length away. The person at the front of the line starts with the ball, passes the ball backwards over their head (up) to the person behind them, this person then passes behind them but this time through their own legs (under).This then continues in alternate ways, up, under, up, under etc. When the person at the back of the line receives it they run to the front of the line and they start again. The winning team is the team that can get everyone round to the front of the line and finish with the person who started, returning to the front.

Topic: Football

Weeks: 6 and 7

Year Group: 1-2

Objectives/Learning Outcomes:
Team Matches.

Special Requirements: Correct footwear and clothes.

Duration: 30 minutes.

Duration: (Minutes)	Activity	Coaching Points	Organisation	Resources/ Equipment
5-10	Cups and Saucers	Working together and being part of a team.	Two teams	Cones
20-30	Small sided matches, progressing to a full match.	Explain: the aim of the game, the parameters, to try and remember the skills, teamwork.	Small sided teams of approx 4-5 players. Eventually two teams.	Balls Bibs Cones Whistle Football pitch (or equivalent)
5	Follow my leader Stretches	Recap good and not so good points	As a class	N/A

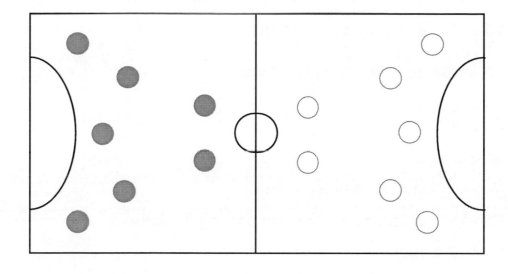

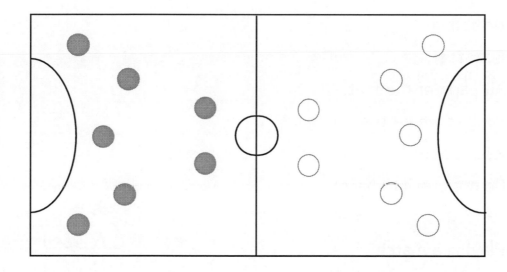

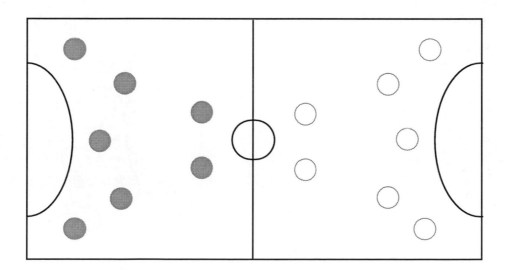

Football - Summary

What have the children learnt?

What are the main points when:

Passing?

Side of the foot.

Non-kicking foot beside the ball.

Non-kicking foot faces the way passing the ball.

Look at target.

Dribbling?

Both feet.

All parts of the foot.

Look at where they are going.

Keep the ball as close to the feet as possible.

Do not use your hands.

Playing a match?

Keeping spread out.

All the above skills.

Working as a team.

Part 2

Years 3 to 6

A - Running

Week 1: The breakdown of sprinting

Warm up:
Ask the class to get into a line. In Week 1 it is explained to them why we need to warm up and how it helps reduce the risk of injury. The class then jog around a given area about the size of a netball court.

Once they have done this, ask the class to get into a circle with a space between each of them, ready to start stretching.

Main Activity:
Running constantly for twenty minutes will not only tire the children but it will also become boring for them, so in order to maintain their concentration the technique for a sprint can be broken down.

Firstly, divide the children into approximately four groups.

Then ask them what is used when we run. Get someone to demonstrate and encourage the answers to include the arms as well as the legs, as the children do not always realise the arms are important when running.

To help both the coach and children, remember the five basic components of a sprint, the initials of each component can be put together to form the word 'S.H.A.R.K.'.

Activity 1: 'S' is for strides

Over the marked out area, encourage the children to bounce from one leg to the other as though they are walking in space with exaggerated strides.

Use the back leg and foot to push off from.

Each child can repeat this two or three times each.

Activity 2: 'H' is for head

The children run as they normally would, focusing on keeping their head high and looking straight ahead of them. Children often feel they are competing against each other when they are running and will usually look over their shoulder to see how the other person is doing, this exercise is to try and minimise this.

A development of this exercise can be to balance quoits on the children's heads whilst they try to run and keep the quoits from falling without using their hands.

Activity 3: 'A' is for arms

Children do not usually realise the importance of using their arms correctly when running. To let them feel the difference, ask the children to run keeping their arms down by their side. Ask them how they felt.

Now the coach demonstrates running with an exaggerated arm movement, making sure the arms are bent and swing close to the body and elbows are tucked in and not outwards.

Chapter 3 - Lesson Plans: Part 2 - Years 3 to 6

Activity 4: 'R' is for remembering to breathe

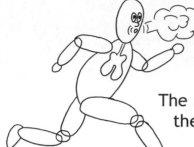

After the children run what is it they can hear? Deep, fast breathing is usually quite common.

The next time the children run, encourage them to take deep breaths in and out.

Activity 5: 'K' is for knees

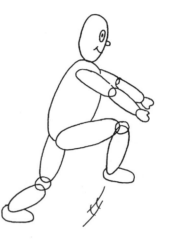

Children now run bringing their knees as high as possible.

To help encourage this they can hold out their hands at waist height and as they run they have to try and touch their hands with their knees (without lowering their hands).

Activity 6: 'S.H.A.R.K.'

Recap all the components of 'S.H.A.R.K.' and let the children see if they can run applying all five together.

Cool down/Summary:
Basic gentle stretches with the whole group. If the group is positioned into a circle they can then interact and discuss what the main coaching points were of the lesson whilst doing a cool down.

Topic: Running

Week: 1

Year Group: 3-6

Objectives/Learning Outcomes:
The breakdown of sprinting.

Special Requirements: Correct footwear and clothes.

Duration: 30 minutes.

Duration: (Minutes)	Activity	Coaching Points	Organisation	Resources/ Equipment
5	Short Jog Stretches	Main muscle groups for running	Circle	Whistle
20	Breakdown sprint Do short bursts with each section	Strides Head High Arms Remember to breathe Knees High	3 or 4 groups	Cones Whistle Baton
5/10	Jog/Walk/ Stretches	Re-Cap **S.H.A.R.K.**	Circle	N/A

Main Activity Layout

S.H.A.R.K.

Strides
Focus on long strides.
Push off back leg.

Head High
Run keeping your head up.
Look where you are going NOT at others.

Arms
Elbows bent, swing arms with run.

Remember to breathe
Run with deep breathing.

Knees High
Run bringing knees up high.

Finally do all of the above together. End with races.

← Netball court approx. 30m →

Group of Children

Group of Children

Group of Children

Week 2: Timing the children sprint

Warm up:
The class jog around a given area about the size of a netball court.
Once they have done this, position the class into a circle with a space between each of them, ready to start stretching.
Can the children remember the exercises?
Can they remember which main muscles are being used?
Bicep, Triceps, Quadriceps, Hamstrings and Gastrocnemius (Calf)

Main Activity:
Divide the children into two groups.
Ask the children to run in their groups, one at a time re-capping 'S.H.A.R.K.'
Tell the children that they are going to be taking part in a test against themselves and not each other. This should help to reduce the concept of competition as they are trying to learn the correct running technique.
The children are going to be timed over a distance of about 60-90 metres, do they know how far athletes run in sprint races? (100m and 200m sprints.)

Children are now put back into one group. Sit the class along the side of the running track, so that they can see those running.
Two adults or children need to stand at the finish line with stopwatches, their job will be to time one child running and recall the finish time to the teacher who will have a list of names and can then record the children's sprint times. (Example in Appendices.)
The teacher calls up two children at a time to sprint, not to race against each other but against time. Each child should run twice and the best time will then be used to compare with the final sprint time in Week 4.
When all the children have completed their two sprints, the whole group lines up and they all sprint against each other.

Cool down/Summary:
Get the children to jog as a group around the track, field etc. and complete some gentle stretches.
It is important to reduce the idea of competition against each other at this age. Explain as much as possible about differences in those that are natural sprinters and others who are natural long distance, endurance runners.

Topic: Running

Week: 2

Year Group: 3-6

Objectives/Learning Outcomes:
To develop correct running styles.

Special Requirements: Correct footwear and clothes.

Duration: 30 minutes.

Duration: (Minutes)	Activity	Coaching Points	Organisation	Resources/ Equipment
5	Gentle Jog Stretches	Explain the muscles being stretched.	As a class	N/A
20	Re-Cap **S.H.A.R.K.** and timed sprinting	**S**trides **H**ead High **A**rms **R**emember to breathe **K**nees High	Small groups to recap S.H.A.R.K. In pairs for sprints	Cones Whistle Stopwatch Sprint record sheet Pen
5	Group jog Stretches	Discuss how they felt being timed. Discuss their sprint times.	As a class in a circle for stretches	Sprint record sheet

Activity 2:

Timed Sprinting

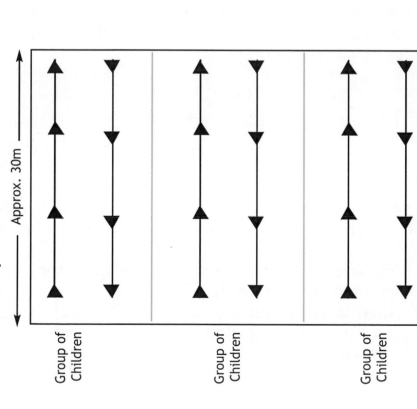

The class sit along the side of the track to observe.

R = Runners   T = Timers

Activity 1:

Recap 'S.H.A.R.K.'

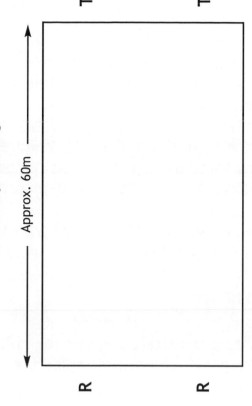

Group of Children

Group of Children

Group of Children

At first each group run carrying out each movement of 'S.H.A.R.K.', one at a time then run combining them all.

Week 3: Baton changing and relay

Warm up:
Jog, walk, jog, sprint.

Around a given area, for example a netball court, get the children to jog along the long sides of the court, walk on one of the short sides and sprint on the other short side.

This can then be followed by stretches. Can any of the children predict what stretches are going to be used? If they can remember the stretches from previous weeks ask the children to demonstrate them. Correct them if necessary.
Refer to pages 6-8 to know what muscle is being stretched for each exercise. Ask the children if they know.

Activity 1: Baton Changing

Children are put into groups of approximately six. Ask the children to stand facing the way they are going to run, not facing the person that is running towards them.

The aim of this exercise is to encourage running and facing the same way you are running. This will also help to develop a correct technique for baton change over.

```
A•          B•          C•          D•          E•
6, 1   →    2    →      3    →      4    →      5 ↓
↑     ←           ←           ←           ←        ↓
```

Two children should stand at cone A (e.g. child 1 and 6) and one child should stand on each of the other cones B,C,D,E.

- ❏ Child 1 starts with the baton and runs to child 2, they exchange the baton at cone B.
- ❏ Child 1 then stays on cone B.
- ❏ Child 2 runs to cone C and gives the baton to child 3.
- ❏ Child 2 stays at cone C.
- ❏ Child 3 runs to cone D and gives the baton to child 4.
- ❏ Child 3 stays at cone D.

- ❏   Child 4 runs to cone E and passes the baton to child 5.
- ❏   Child 4 stays at cone E.
- ❏   Child 5 then runs back to the start to give the baton to child 6.
- ❏   Child 5 stays at cone A.
- ❏   Child 6 then runs to cone B to pass the baton over to child 1,
- ❏   Child 6 stays at this cone
- ❏   Child 1 then runs to child 2, and so on.

The runner who receives the baton needs to have their arm out behind them with the palm of their hand facing upwards, and with their back turned to the person who is approaching them.

On receiving the baton, the receiving runner should grip the baton firmly and run with the baton using it in their stride.

Activity 2: Relay Race

Spread each group out at a realistic distance between each runner, perhaps 40-60m.

Encourage the children to use the 'S.H.A.R.K.' technique as well as the new baton exchange they have just been practising.

Activity 3: Starting position

On your marks, get set, go!

Introduce the starting position professional athlete's use when racing.

Step 1: On your marks

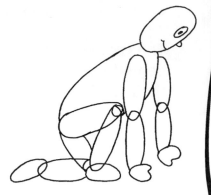

Hands should be on the starting line and arms should be shoulder width apart.

Legs should be directly out behind each hand with knees bent.

Step 2: Get set

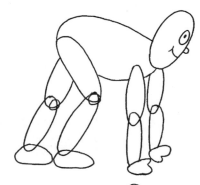

Keeping the original position, on this mark you simply push your bottom up into the air, and extend the arms and legs slightly.

Step 3: Go!

Push off using the legs and pull yourself upright, and start 'S.H.A.R.K'.

Cool Down/Summary:
Get the children to jog as a group around the track, field etc. and complete some gentle stretches.

Teachers should again emphasise at this point it is not a race, but it is to practise a correct technique for both running and baton exchange.

Topic: Running

Week: 3

Year Group: 3-6

Objectives/Learning Outcomes:
To learn the correct techniques for baton exchange.

Special Requirements: Correct footwear and clothes.

Duration: 30 minutes.

Duration: (Minutes)	Activity	Coaching Points	Organisation	Resources/ Equipment
5	Sprint, jog, walk	Can the children remember the main muscles?	As a class	N/A
20	Baton exchange Relay race	Remember S.H.A.R.K. when running. Hand out when receiving. Hand over has to be sensible so the baton isn't dropped.	Class divided into 3 groups. Relay Race in 2 teams	Cones Whistle Batons
5	Stretches	Discuss technique	As a class in a circle for stretches.	N/A

Activity 1: Baton Exchange

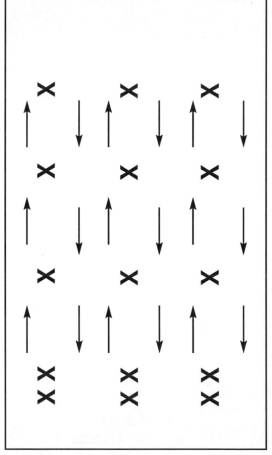

Practise change over of baton.

Face the way in which you are going to run, not the person who is running towards you.

Hold hand out behind, palm upwards, ready to receive the baton.

Once the person with the baton has handed it over, they stand where the person they gave the baton to was standing. They then turn around, ready to receive the baton and run back to their original place.

Warm up

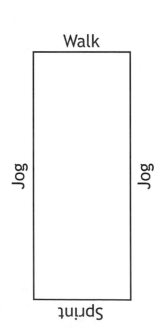

Walk along one width of the track and sprint on the other width.

Relay Race

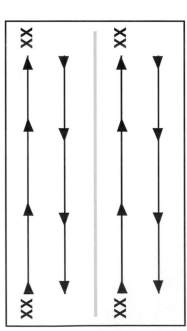

A race between 2 teams
Encourage the children to look where they are running!

Week 4: Second week of timed sprints

Warm up:
Jog, walk, jog, walk. Followed by stretches.
Can any of the children lead the stretches with prompts?

Activity 1: Baton Relay

Recap previous baton exchange coaching points and repeat last week's activity, practising the change over. Children can then have a relay race in their teams.
Emphasise 'H' of 'S.H.A.R.K.', as children will tend to look at where the other children are when they are racing instead of keeping their head high and looking at where they are running to. Also explain it helps them run faster if they look where they are going.

Activity 2: Timed Sprints

As in Week 2, arrange the children along the side of the running track so that they can see other children running.
Explain again to the children that they will be carrying out two sprints each, to compete only against themselves and time instead of against each other.
The scores they get this week will then be compared to their best time in Week 2, to see if they have improved.
Again two children or adults need to be positioned at the end of the finish line with stopwatches and a record sheet.
Each child runs twice and the best time is taken. To reduce fatigue, it is best that the children do their first run and then complete their second run once everyone has had their first go. Once all the children have run twice and their results have been collected, compare the scores.

Are there any patterns?
Who has improved?
Who has stayed the same?
Are there reasons why some children may have got slower times?

Cool down/Summary:
Get the children to jog as a group around the track, field etc. and complete some gentle stretches.

Topic: Running

Week: 4

Year group: 3-6

Objectives/Learning Outcomes:
Comparing timed sprints to Week 2 results.

Special Requirements: Correct footwear and clothes.

Duration: 30 minutes.

Duration: (Minutes)	Activity	Coaching Points	Organisation	Resources/ Equipment
5	Jog, walk, jog Stretches	Can the children remember the main muscles?	Around track	N/A
20	Recap the baton relay Timed sprints	Hand out Look where they are running to S.H.A.R.K.	In 3 groups for relay practice In pairs for sprints	Cones Whistle Batons Stopwatch Sprint record sheet pen
5	Group jog Stretches	Discuss why there might be differences between the two sets of results.	As a class in a circle for stretches	Sprint record sheet

Activity 2: Timed Sprinting

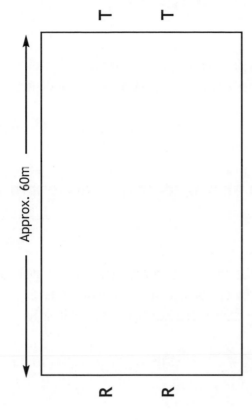

Approx. 60m

R   R

T   T

The class sit along the side of the track to observe.

R = Runners   T = Timers

Warm up

Jog

Walk   Walk

Jog

Walk the lengths of the track.
Jog the widths of the tracks.

Activity 1: Relay Race

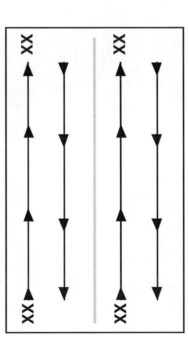

XX   XX

XX   XX

A race between 2 teams
Encourage them to look where they are running!

Week 5-7: Practising techniques

Main activity:
Now that the basics of S.H.A.R.K. have been taught, the final weeks of running lessons can be used to repeat the previous weeks.
Races between the children can include starting in the 'On your marks, Get set, Go' positions (see page 64).

Can the children develop their running techniques and improve their sprint times?

Cool down/Summary:
Children jog, walk and alternate these movements. Also get them to change direction. In between changes of movement the children can carry out a gentle stretch. Recap main muscle areas.

Running - Summary

What have the children learnt?

What does S.H.A.R.K. stand for?

Strides
Head High
Arms
Remember to breathe
Knees High

Can the children practise and improve their times?
What do the children think is the most important factor
of S.H.A.R.K.?
Is there a most important factor?
If so, why?
What have the children learnt?
What did they find hard?
What was easy?

When exchanging the baton what way should you look?
The way you are going to run.

B - Football

Week 1: Basic Football skills

Warm up:
Short jog and numbers game.
Stretches.

Main activity: Skills circuit
The circuit should be laid out as on the activity layout on page 77.
The circuit is broken down into three main skills: heading, passing
and dribbling.

Activity 1: Heading

When teaching to head a football, the main emphasis should be to
keep your eyes open and use the forehead. These two factors will
then minimise heading the ball causing any pain or discomfort,
which most children are afraid of.

Once the correct heading technique has been demonstrated, as
well as making a point that the throw needs to be decent, the
children then need to be put into pairs, where one should gently
throw the ball and the other 'head' the ball back.

The children take this in turns, (head about five times and then
swap).
For those who are scared perhaps start throwing from a very short
distance. This means the ball is literally just dropped instead of
thrown, their confidence should grow as they realise it doesn't hurt.
The distance is then slowly increased and eventually the child
heading the ball can do so from a distance. The main part of this
activity is to decrease the fear of heading.

Some children who have experience in football will find this
activity easier than those with no experience. If this is the case,
the children can practise aiming to head the ball directly to the
thrower's hands every time.

If they can complete this with ease, get them to help those who
are struggling with the activity.

Activity 2: Passing

Children are again in pairs and simply pass the ball to each other.

Demonstrate the correct technique before they start. The main points to consider are; the correct part of the kicking foot, where the non-kicking foot goes, to use accuracy not power, and to look where they are kicking the ball.

The correct part of the foot should be the instep when passing. Point to the area of the foot and get the children in the group to touch their insteps with their hand. Check that all the children are holding the correct part of their foot as this will help them remember.

The non-kicking foot is just as important as the kicking foot and is placed next to the ball when kicking the ball. The toes of the non-kicking foot should point in the direction the ball is being kicked.

When the child receives the ball, emphasise the importance of first getting the ball under control before passing the ball back. Stop the ball, again using their instep, and then adjust themselves so that they are in the correct position to pass the ball back using the correct technique.

Some children find this easier than others, so for those that have difficulty, encourage them to swing their leg as though it is a golf club, but keeping their leg slightly bent. For the more advanced, explain about keeping the knee over the ball when striking it so that the ball is kept lower to the ground.

A simple development could be for children to learn the basic stop and pass using both feet, a skill that is very valuable within the game.

A development also for the more experienced and older children can be to tap the ball to one side of their body when receiving the ball ready to pass straight back to their partner, instead of stopping the ball dead.

Activity 3: Dribbling

Dribbling around the cones helps to develop good footwork. The best way to develop dribbling skills is to encourage the use of both feet and all areas of the foot.

The children should start by walking the ball with their feet around the cones and back again. It is important to encourage the children not to use their hands when they feel they are loosing control of the ball.

Children will probably tend to watch the floor instead of where they are going, so encourage them to keep their 'Heads High'.

The class needs to be divided as equally as possible between the three stations, and they spend between five to seven minutes on each.

If the children do not manage all three stations the activity can be repeated. It is usually a good idea to run this activity over two weeks, so that during the first week each station can be explained fully, and in the second, children will get longer to practise each activity in more depth.

Cool down/Summary:
Basic gentle stretches with the whole group. If the group is positioned into a circle they can then interact and discuss what the main coaching points were of the lesson whilst doing a cool down.

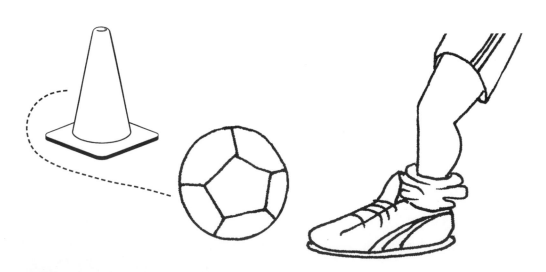

Week 2: Skills circuit

Everything this week is as Week 1. However, the initial introduction should have made the children aware of what they need to do, so this week's introduction is just a brief reminder of each station.

The coach can now reinforce all the main coaching points for each station. For those children that feel that the task has become too easy, they can develop their non-dominant foot on the dribbling and passing tasks, and can perfect their heading skills.

Cool down/Summary:
Basic gentle stretches with the whole group. If the group is positioned into a circle they can then interact and discuss what the main coaching points were of the lesson whilst doing a cool down.

Topic: Football

Week: 1 and 2

Year Group: 3-6

Objectives/Learning Outcomes:
To understand football skills.

Special Requirements: Correct footwear and clothes.

Duration: 40 minutes.

Duration: (Minutes)	Activity	Coaching Points	Organisation	Resources/ Equipment
5-10	Short jog with numbers Stretches	1 = Left hand down 2 = Right hand down 3 = Jump 4 = Change direction **Main muscle groups for football**	Circle	N/A
20-30	Passing Control/ Dribbling Headers	- Inside of foot - Look up - Use both feet - Eyes open - Use forehead	Partners and small groups	Cones Whistle Footballs
5	Stretches	Re-cap above	Circle	N/A

Main Activities

Layout of cones

Passing

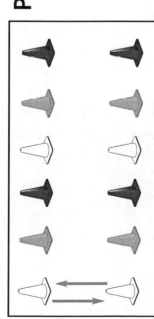

Passing

- Use side of the foot.
- Stop the ball before passing back.
- Those that find this too easy, stop the ball to the side and pass back. (Coach to demonstrate.)
- Non kicking foot next to the ball, and face the way you want to kick.

Heading

Heading

- In pairs.
- Throw ball to player who heads it back.
- Use forehead.
- Keep eyes OPEN.

Dribbling

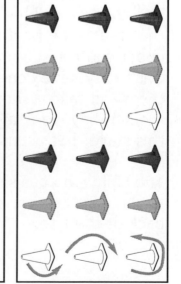

Dribbling

Dribble ball around cones:
- Right Foot,
- Left Foot,
- Both,
- Use all parts of both feet.

Week 3: Combining skills

Warm up:
High and Low Fives.
Stretches.

Main activity:
Using the knowledge of Weeks 1 and 2, the skills can now be combined together, slowly showing how the skills can be used in a match situation, when lots of skills are mixed together in various orders.
Again to keep a variety within the lesson, a skills circuit is used. Three stations are set up, a different activity being carried out at each of them.

Activity 1: Dribble and Pass

The children demonstrate their previous dribbling skills in and out of the cones. However, instead of dribbling the ball back around the cones, when the children reach the end cone, they turn, get the ball in the correct position and pass the ball back to the next person. This time the coaching points need to emphasise stopping the ball and getting it under control before passing it or before starting to dribble with it. The techniques for dribbling and passing are exactly the same as learnt previously.
Once they have passed the ball back they then jog back to the end of the line, being careful not to get in the next player's way.

Activity 2: Dribble and Shoot

The children dribble the ball in and out of the cones and when they reach the final cone, they should stop the ball and get it under control.
Once they have done this they should look at the target in front of them and take a shot aiming the ball between the two cones, as though they were taking a shot at goal. Power is not essential at this stage, but accuracy is.

The child who has shot then needs to collect the ball and run back to the next person, and hands the ball over before joining the back of the line.

Activity 3: Pass and Move

The children in their set groups need to be put into smaller groups of three in this activity. Each three then need to go to a square, which will already be set up according to the plan. The aim is to practise passing to each other in their square. However, once they pass the ball they need to run to the spare cone. This will encourage the children to run into a space after passing the ball, and hopefully stop the children remaining static when in a game situation.

The techniques for this activity are exactly as before when passing. The children need to remember to stop and control the ball before passing it back.

Cool down/Summary:
Instruct the children to jog around in a given area avoiding any equipment and each other. When an instruction is given the children should then carry it out. For example, if 'Girls and blue cones' is called, all the girls walk (or whatever move has been stated) to a blue cone and return it to a place that they have been told to put it.

To minimise any bumps you can then state that they must walk around in spaces, and perhaps when calling the instruction you can limit it to certain people; for example, people with blue eyes, etc. Make sure that everyone gets a turn. This is also a great way to get the children to pack the equipment away at the end of a session.

Topic: Football

Week: 3

Year Group: 3-6

Objectives/Learning Outcomes:
To combine the basic skills.

Special Requirements: Correct footwear and clothes.

Duration: 40 minutes.

Duration: (Minutes)	Activity	Coaching Points	Organisation	Resources/ Equipment
5-10	High and Low Fives Stretches	Emphasise high or low to move the whole body.	As a class in a large space	Whistle
20-30	Dribble and Pass Dribble and Shoot Pass and Move	Describe each activity. Techniques exactly the same as when the skills are carried out individually.	In groups divided over each activity	Cones Whistle Footballs
5	Gentle jog	What other skills can be mixed? e.g. pass and shoot	As a class	N/A

Field Layout

1. Dribble and Pass

2. Dribble and Shoot

3 Pass and Move

◁ = Cone

Week 4 and 5: To use previous skills in a match situation

Warm up:
Cups and Saucers.

Main activity:
The class need to be divided into small teams. A suitable number would be five to seven in each team.

Before going into a match situation, give each team a ball and let them practise passing within their team.

After a little practice put two teams per pitch. At this stage, it is advised not to go straight into a normal match situation, as some players may get left out, children tend to bunch around the ball and all the previously learnt skills seem to get forgotten.

To minimise any of the above from happening, set rules can be introduced to the match.

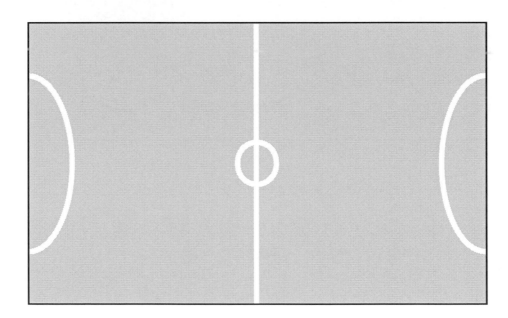

Game 1:

In order for a goal to be scored and counted, set in place a certain number of passes that have to be completed before scoring. For example, four passes have to be made before an attempt at goal. These can be either four consecutive passes, or just a total of four passes before each shot.

This should help encourage passing within the team and teamwork, it will also help minimise the more able from doing all the work themselves.

Game 2:

Allow only three touches per person at one time. This is to encourage stopping the ball, getting it under control and passing or shooting. It also prevents any of the more able players being selfish with the ball and encourages team work.

These are only a couple of ideas to introduce into the game to encourage passing and teamwork, and can also help everyone get involved.

Cool down/Summary:
Emphasize how important teamwork and communication are. For example they need to let the person behind them know what way they are passing the ball.
Children are put into teams in lines one behind the other. Making sure that the person in front is about arms length away. The person at the front of the line starts with the ball, passes the ball backwards over their head (up) to the person behind them, this person then passes behind them but this time through their own legs (under). This then continues in alternate ways up, under, up, under etc. When the person at the back of the line receives it they run to the front of the line and they start again. The winning team is the team that can get everyone round to the front of the line and finish when the person who started with the ball has returned to the front.

Topic: Football

Week: 4 and 5

Year Group: 3-6

Objectives/Learning Outcomes:
To use previous skills in a team and match situation.

Special Requirements: Correct footwear and clothes.

Duration: 40 minutes.

Duration: (Minutes)	Activity	Coaching Points	Organisation	Resources/ Equipment
5-10	Cups and Saucers Stretches	Working and being a part of a team	Two teams	Cones Whistle
20-30	Match situations: - Set Passes - 3 touches	'x' number of passes have to be made before scoring. 3 touches at a time per person and then pass or shoot.	Small sided teams e.g. 5-a-side	Cones Whistle Footballs
5	Stretches Up Under game	Discuss performances	As a class	N/A

Match Situation

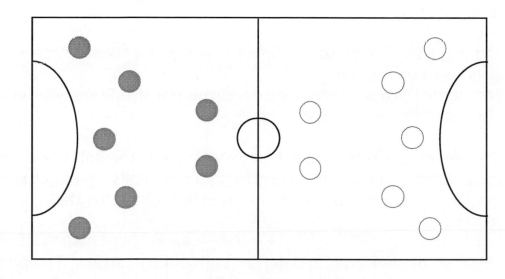

Team 1 •
Team 2 ○

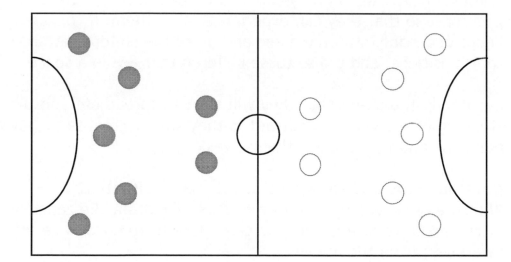

Week 6 and 7: Spatial awareness in a full match situation

Warm up:
Cups and Saucers.

Main activity:
The children should now have some very basic skills for football, and will have gained some idea of working in a team within a given area on a pitch.
The biggest problem when introducing a full size Primary level pitch is the children's use of space.

The perception is that the children will follow the ball wherever it goes. To help minimise this and to help the pupils develop their spatial awareness, put them into three groups within their teams.

They can be divided into defence, midfield and attack. The pitch is then divided into three sections. This will also help gain an idea of positions in football.

Explain to each group where their area is and that they are allowed anywhere within that area.
Throughout the lesson they can be swapped over into the other positions, so that they can experience all of them. If 'bunching' keeps occurring, stop the game and make the children aware of their positions, and praise those children that are in a space.

Eventually the aim is that they will start to spread out and the stopping of the game is reduced as they start to realise if they are bunching and find a space themselves.

Developments and variations to the match situation:
With the older year groups or more able children, the zones of the pitch can be removed from the game sooner, to encourage spatial awareness from themselves.

The pitch can also be divided into more zones, introducing left and right to the three original zones, which will minimise dribbling but would encourage passing the ball in more directions instead of just forward and back.

Years 5 and 6 can be introduced to some basic rules of the game.
- Instead of just throwing the ball back into play, more of an understanding can be taught about the correct technique of a throw in.
- Goal kicks and corners can be explained.
- Set play.
- Goal keeper's rules.

By the final week in the later years see if the children can play a normal game and still use the spatial awareness, although they are allowed in any area.

Cool down/Summary:
'Copy this, Copy that' is a great way of getting the children to cool down and to encourage listening skills.
If the leader says an instruction such as 'Copy this' and jogs on the spot, then children should copy the movement. If they sprint and say 'Copy that' the children should carry on jogging on the spot. This is very similar to Simon says, but because it is a cool down activity, the movements should not be too strenuous.

Topic: Football

Week: 6 and 7

Year Group: 3-6

Objectives/Learning Outcomes:
To develop spatial awareness in a match situation.

Special Requirements: Correct footwear and clothes.

Duration: 40 minutes.

Duration: (Minutes)	Activity	Coaching Points	Organisation	Resources/ Equipment
5-10	Cups and saucers Stretches	Working and being a part of a team	Two teams	Cones Whistle
20-30	Creating spatial awareness in a match situation	Recap skills and the importance of still using them. Give each player a specific zone, attack, midfield and defence.	The class is divided into two teams. Each team is then split into zones.	Cones Whistle Footballs
5	Stretches Copy this, Copy that game	Discuss areas, and why is it imortant to space out.	As a class	N/A

Pitch Layout

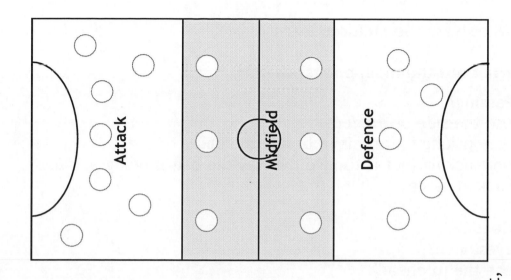

ZONE 1

ZONE 2

ZONE 3

Defence

Midfield

Attack

Attack

Midfield

Defence

TEAM

◯ Shoot ←

● Shoot →

NOTE
This is how both
teams are set out,
all on one pitch

Football - Summary

Do any of the children stand out from the rest?

Why? In what way?

What have the children learnt?

What are the main points when:

Passing?
Use the side of the foot
Non-kicking foot remains beside the ball
Non-kicking foot is to face the way the ball is being passed
Look at target

Heading?
Eyes open
Use the forehead

Dribbling?
Both feet
All parts of the foot
Look at where you are going
Keep the ball as close to the feet as possible
Do not use your hands

Playing a match?
Keeping spread out
All the above skills
Working as a team

C - Kwik Cricket

Week 1: Basic throw and catch skills

Warm up:
Focus on arms.
High and low fives.

Activity 1: Chasing the ball

Put the class into groups of 4-6.
The person at the front of the line (person A) rolls the ball towards the cone. It is the aim that the person next in line runs and stops the ball before it reaches the cone and then rolls the ball back to person A, and then joins the back of the line.
Person A is then next to chase the ball and so on.

Coaching points:

When stopping the ball make sure you bend your knees. And if you try and stop the ball with your feet there is a risk that you will stand on the ball and fall, so it is best to try and stop the ball using your hands.

The person who rolls it for the next person to chase, needs to roll it gently.

When rolling the ball remember accuracy is more important than power.

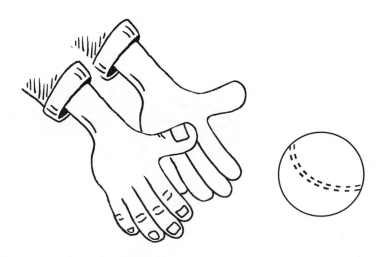

Activity 2: Throwing and catching in a circle

In their groups children practise throwing to each other and catching. The aim of this is to work as a team, not to try and catch each other out.

For better accuracy start the children off by using under arm throwing.

When catching the ball demonstrate the correct technique, by using both hands and cushioning the catch by drawing it in towards your body.

Activity 3: Throwing and catching in two groups

Divide the class into two groups and stand them in two lines facing each other. Start the distance between them at about 1m. The person at the front throws to the person at the front of the other line, and then joins the back of the line.

Once the two groups can all throw and catch the ball without dropping it, increase the distance between the two groups. The aim is that eventually each group is a big distance apart and they can practise long distance throwing.

If they manage to get the distance increased they may need to change their under arm throw to over arm. Again the catching technique is to cushion the ball in towards the body.

Cool down/Summary:
Basic gentle stretches with the whole group. If the group is positioned into a circle they can then interact and discuss what the main coaching points were of the lesson whilst doing a cool down.

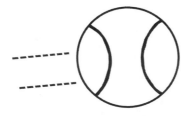

Topic: Kwik Cricket

Week: 1

Year Group: 3-6

Objectives/Learning Outcomes:
To learn a basic throw and catch.

Special Requirements: Correct footwear and clothes.

Duration: 30 minutes.

Duration: (Minutes)	Activity	Coaching Points	Organisation	Resources/ Equipment
5-10	High and Low Fives Stretches	Focus on arms and back	As a class	N/A
20-30	Roll and stop Basic throw and catch. Team throwing and catching with various distances.	Use both hands to catch. Bring the ball in towards the body to cushion it. Look at where throwing it to.	Small groups Pairs Two groups	Cones Whistle Tennis balls/ Cricket balls
5	Gentle jog Stretches	Recap coaching points for throwing	As a class	N/A

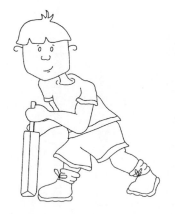

Activity 2: Practise throwing and catching

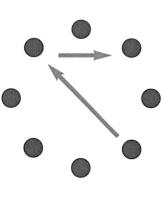

Children practise throwing and catching stood in a circle.

Children stand in 2 groups, the person at the front throws the ball and moves to the back of the line, the person opposite receives the ball, throws it back and joins the back of their line etc.

Activity 1: Roll and stop

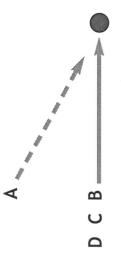

A

D C B

Person B rolls the ball forwards, Person A runs and stops the ball.

D C B

A

Person A then rolls the ball back to B and joins the line.

B

A D C

B then gets ready to run after the ball when C rolls it, and so on . . . .

Week 2: Bowling skills for under and over arm

Warm up:
- Upper arm, lower arm and back.
- Beans

Main activity:
Divide the children into equal groups on each of the wicket stations.
One person stands as back stop behind one of the wickets, and their job is to collect the ball and roll it back to the next person.

Rolling:
Start by rolling the ball at the wickets. Remind the children that accuracy is more important than power. Ask the children to think about how their body feels when the ball is being rolled, and how their body is positioned. Again bend the knees when bowling and swing the arm so that there is enough power for the ball to reach the wickets.

Under arm bowl:
Demonstrate an under arm bowl to begin with, making sure the ball bounces before hitting the wickets. The best technique is to have the leg opposite to that of the throwing arm forward and to use the non-throwing arm as guidance.
Children then take it in turns to bowl at the wickets. Once they have taken their bowl they join the back of the line as the wicket keeper collects the ball. Once everyone in the group has had a turn the wicket keeper changes over, so that children can experience both roles.

Over arm throw:
Demonstrate an over arm throw, remembering to use the non throwing arm as a guide, making sure the ball bounces before hitting the wickets. Give the children a target that is just before the wickets, perhaps the crease, and tell them to aim their throw so that the ball bounces around that point to give a better aim at the wickets.

Cool down/Summary:
Basic gentle stretches with the whole group. If the group is positioned into a circle they can then interact and discuss what the main coaching points were of the lesson whilst doing a cool down.

Topic: Kwik Cricket

Week: 2

Year Group: 3-6

Objectives/Learning Outcomes:
To learn a basic throw and catch.

Special Requirements: Correct footwear and clothes.

Duration: 30 minutes.

Duration: (Minutes)	Activity	Coaching Points	Organisation	Resources/ Equipment
5-10	Beans Stretches	Focus on upper arm. What muscles are used in the bowling action? *(Bicep and Tricep)*	As a class	N/A
20-30	Aiming at the wickets: - Rolling - Under arm - Over arm	Accuracy not power. Just enough power to make the ball reach the wickets. Explain each bowling action. Over arm: accuracy before power.	Small groups Taking in turns as backstop	Cones Whistle Tennis balls/ Cricket balls Wickets
5	Stretches	Discuss each action, easiest - hardest?	As a class	N/A

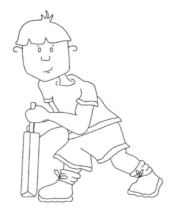

Each person takes a turn to bowl.

The backstop collects the ball and rolls it back to the next person.

Once everyone has taken a bowl, the person to bowl first swaps place with the backstop, allowing everyone a go in backstop and bowl.

Notes for over arm bowling:

Fingers over crease on the ball (see below).

Use non-bowling arm as a guide.

Aim to bounce the ball just in front of the wickets.

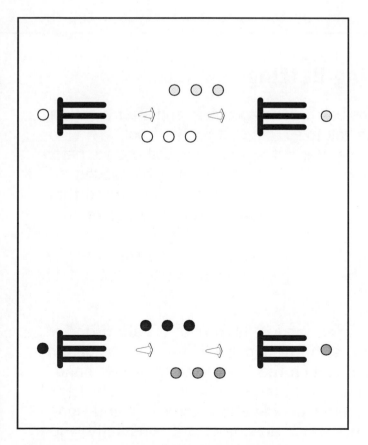

○ = Group 1   standing positions

◉ = Group 2   standing positions

○ = Group 3   standing positions

● = Group 4   standing positions

▷ = Cones for bowling points

Ⅲ = Wickets

Week 3: Batting skills

Warm up:
Upper arm, lower arm and back.
Cups and Saucers

Main activity:
Questions for the children.
What are two types of batting technique that could be used in cricket? *Attacking and defensive.*
Explain and demonstrate the correct way for holding a bat.
The dominant hand grips the bottom and the other the top. Hold the bat at the dominant side of the body and stand side ways on towards the bowler.
Divide the class equally on each wicket station. One person goes in bat whilst the other bowls. The children take 'x' number of goes each and swap so that they get a chance to practise their bowling as well as their batting.

Activity 1: Defensive Batting

No swing is included when defending the wickets, the aim is to stop the ball from hitting the wicket, and to keep the ball down low to avoid being caught out.
As the batsperson hits the ball, the aim for this activity is to tap the ball back to the bowler.

Activity 2: Attacking Batting

This time the aim is to hit the ball as far as possible, and after practising knowing where you want the ball to go, direct it to that 'spot'.
As the ball is thrown, sometimes it is better to let the ball bounce before hitting it, or if the throw is too hard a defensive bat may be needed.
For this exercise it is important that the children understand that when they bowl they have to try and bowl so that the person in bat can hit the ball.
As the ball travels towards the batsperson, it may be that they need to move and adjust their body in order to hit the ball better.

Cool down/Summary:
Gentle movements into an area, and if 'high five' is called find a partner and high-five them, same to happen if 'low five' is called. If 'left hand' down is called, touch the floor with their left hand and continue moving around space, same to happen if 'right hand' is called. This should get them thinking about their left and right and high and low movements which are important especially when fielding in cricket.

Topic: Kwik Cricket

Week: 3

Year Group: 3-6

Objectives / Learning Outcomes:
Basic Batting Skills.

Special Requirements: Correct footwear and clothes.

Duration: 30 minutes.

Duration: (Minutes)	Activity	Coaching Points	Organisation	Resources/ Equipment
5-10	Cups and Saucers Stretches	Focus on upper arms, sides and back.	As a class	N/A
20-30	Batting: - Defensive - Attacking	- Aim to block wickets, not to hit as far as possible. - Aim to hit the ball as far as possible to gain runs.	Small groups Bowler Backstop Batsperson	Cones Whistle Tennis balls/ Cricket balls Wickets Bats
5	Stretch and recap	Fast bowl = defensive hit Slow bowl = attack hit	As a class	N/A

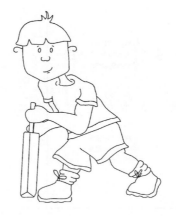

Defensive Batting:

- Bowler takes a bowl
- Batsperson defends the wicket
- Ball is collected by person next to bowl, who is next in line behind the bowler.
- Bowler becomes next batsperson
- Batsperson becomes backstop
- Backstop joins the back of the line

Attacking Batting:

- Each person has the ball bowled under arm to them, they have 2/3 chances to hit an attacking ball.
- The children waiting to bat act as fielders.
- Children to share bowler and backstop positions.

N.B.: Flat marker cones can be positioned in areas fielders should be standing.

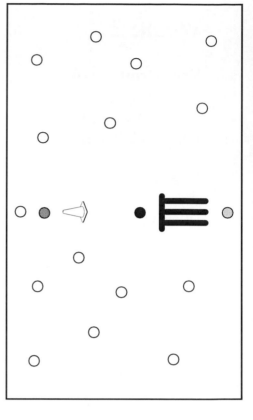

Defensive Batting Layout

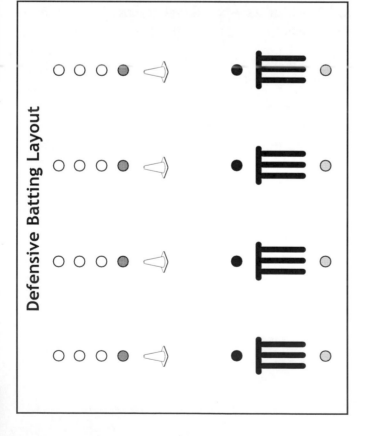

○ = Those waiting

● = Bowler

● = Batsperson

○ = Backstop

◁ = Cones to bowl from

Ⅲ = Wickets

Week 4-7: Putting previous skills learnt into practise

Warm up:
Arms, legs and back.
Cups and Saucers.

Main activity:
The children have now learnt the basic skills of kwik cricket. Before putting them straight into a game situation it is a good idea to introduce the layout of fielders within a game. To make this easier, lay out cones around the pitch where you would want fielders to stand. The fielding team then find a cone each and always have to return to that cone when the bowler has received the ball.

Explain about not all going for the ball, but to only go for the ball if it is hit near their cone. Also if they get the ball the aim is to get the ball back to the bowler, and then as they get used to the rules they can be introduced to trying to get the ball at the wickets if a batsperson is running.

Encourage teamwork. The children should try and use the different types of bowling and batting. Once they have all had a fair amount of time practising fielding with the cones, they can be taken out of the game.

Emphasise the importance of spacing when fielding.

Variations:
When the ball has been hit, each player on the fielding team must throw and receive the ball before it is returned to the bowler.

One or two people on the batting side against everyone else, and when they are out they swap with someone on the fielding team.

Cool down/Summary:
Gentle jogging into a designated area, moving in the way which is instructed. It is a good idea to keep the movements slow and not too intense as it is a cool down exercise, but it can include stretches and moves of left, right, up and down which are all important ways of moving when playing cricket.

Topic: Kwik Cricket

Week: 4-7

Year Group: 3-6

Objectives/Learning Outcomes:
To use basic Kwik Cricket skills in a match situation.

Special Requirements: Correct footwear and clothes.

Duration: 30 minutes.

Duration: (Minutes)	Activity	Coaching Points	Organisation	Resources/ Equipment
5-10	Cups and Saucers Stretches	All areas of stretching	Two teams As a class	Cones
20-30	A match of Kwik Cricket	Explain the rules of Kwik Cricket. Teamwork. Fielding strategies - aim to return ball to bowler. Recap all skills.	Two teams: -Batting -Fielding (Teams will swap, once batting team have all batted)	Cones Whistle Tennis balls/ Cricket balls Wickets Bats
5	Group jog Gentle stretches	What have they learnt?	As a class	N/A

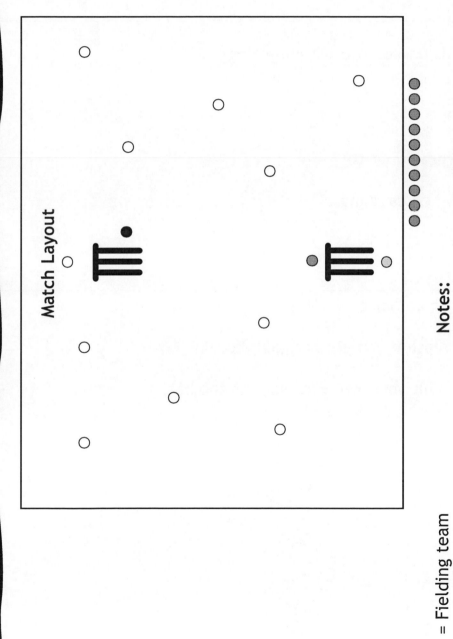

Match Layout

Notes:
- Layout cones where fielding team should stand, to encourage spatial awareness.
- Explain the rules.
- Start with under arm bowling and develop to using over arm bowling once the children have got used to batting.

○ = Fielding team

● = Batting team

● = Backstop

● = Bowler

Ⅲ = Wickets

Kwik Cricket - Summary

What are the main types of bowling action used?

Under arm and over arm.

What are the two types of batting action?

Defensive and attacking.

How many hands do you use when batting?

Two.

When fielding remember to:

Use two hands when catching.

Stand in spaces.

When batting remember to:

Remain in the crease if you are not going to run.

Be careful not to hit your own wickets with the bat.

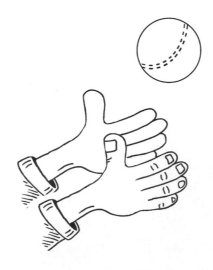

Chapter 4

Cool Down Ideas

At the end of every session a cool down can be just as important as warming up the muscles to help avoid injury.

Gentle stretches and calming games are ideal at Primary age. The aim of these games is to reduce the heart rate and to help calm the children down after a fun session. A great example of this is sleeping lions.

The children lie down on their backs with their arms by their sides and try to remain as still as possible. After a few minutes they sit up slowly, then line up in turn.

Whilst the children are lying down the teacher can talk to them about how the air goes in through their bodies, or tell any relaxing story to help them think about how their body is relaxing.

Calming games are generally easy, slow games that help the children cool down instead of just finishing a fun, lively session and going straight back to class.

The important thing as well as the physical cool down is the discussion and summary time at the end of each lesson. Use the cool down time to discuss performances, show good examples if the children are happy to demonstrate.

Get the children who have taken part in the activity to interact with the discussions. How did they feel? What have they learnt? Sometimes the cool down is the ideal time to recap the main coaching points and to give the children ways to remember them, such as 'S.H.A.R.K.' in running. This can then be their last thought of the session, ready for the next.

The cool down activities do not have to be linked with the theme of the lesson. However, if they do, this is an advantage and helps the lesson to flow. At the end of each lesson there are ideas for what the cool down could consist of and these can be adapted to suit the group. Some of these ideas are repeated throughout the book, however they are easily adaptable to make the actual exercises involved different every time.

Chapter 5

Worksheets

Introduction

The worksheets can be used when the weather does not permit play to be carried out. They can be used instead, or as part of P.E. sessions. The picture worksheets are mainly used for lower age groups/abilities, such as Years 1 to 4. The wordsearches are aimed at the more developed ages such as Years 5 and 6.

Worksheet Criteria for different year groups

Years 1 and 2
- Small groups.
- Give words to use to label picture.
- Explain the picture and each word.
- Talk through each word.

Years 3 and 4
- Do as class activity or in small groups.
- Give each child an answer sheet.
- Put words on the board.
- Explain they have to match the words to the picture and label.
- Talk through answers as a group.

Years 5 and 6
- Do as a class activity or in small groups.
- Give each child an answer sheet.
- Put answers and extra words on the board.
- Get children to label the picture.
- Go through answers as a group.

More Advanced
- Give blank answer sheet and ask to label.
- Go through answers.

General Points:
- Ask why they give answers they do.
- Ask ways they can remember the correct answers, visual clues, e.g.: In football the only person to have a whistle is the referee.
- Get them to compare answers and see why they agree/disagree.

Worksheet 1

Running Wordsearch

Can you find these words that are important in running in the grid below?

ARMS	STRIDES	KNEES
SPRINT	HEAD HIGH	RELAY
RUNNING	RESPIRATION	SHARK

```
G O R E S P I R A T I O N G S D
E A D R K S P D M N O I A B F G
E C Y A N T I R U T D N G Y K K
P P G P E N A U S R T E B O U L
E F B T L E H N Y P E S F N F S
R R D K D T A N J B L T L F B L
F E S R C V E I U A N R M C O I
C H F H P I T N R E T I S J K A
L K E U D E F G N S E D R K T D
M I M A O B Y H G N E U B L F
O P N F D O T B I N L S D F P N
W K H T N H L Z S I G D S A I W
N O N L D P I E T H H M O R T S
S Z F S O I N G A G A G E K G P
B H I P Q U Y T H T C R P J R O
S M A L A V Q O E O D G K G E K
K D I R U N S P R I N T R I L T
G R F R H I K J D U M T S N A R
J T G E U B O H O T N M T C Y E
P O K N H N K N E E S W S R T F
I O N A G R N O G H R V Q O T O
D S T R D K M L P S N F L D S E
F N O M S Y V T D C H K I S E D
S P E S E L V Y N O L F G H T D
```

Running Wordsearch

Can you find these words that are important in running in the grid below?

ARMS	STRIDES	KNEES
SPRINT	HEAD HIGH	RELAY
RUNNING	RESPIRATION	SHARK

```
G O R E S P I R A T I O N G S D
E A D R K S P D M N O I A B F G
E C Y A N T I R U T D N G Y K K
P P G P E N A U S R T E B O U L
E F B T L E H N Y P E S F N F S
R R D K D T A N J B L T L F B L
F E S R C V E I U A N R M C O I
C H F H P I T N R E T I S J K A
L K E U D E F G N S E D R K T D
M I M A O B Y H G H N E U B L F
O P N F D O T B I N L S D F P N
W K H T N H L Z S I G D S A I W
N O N L D P I E T H H M O R T S
S Z F S O I N G A G A G E K G P
B H I P Q U Y T H T C R P J R O
S M A L A V Q O E O D G K G E K
K D I R U N S P R I N T R I L T
G R F R H I K J D U M T S N A R
J T G E U B O H O T N M T C Y E
P O K N H N K N E E S W S R T F
I O N A G R N O G H R V Q O T O
D S T R D K M L P S N F L D S R
F N O M S Y V T D C H K I S E E
S P E S E L V Y N O L F G H T D
```

Worksheet 2

Running

During your P.E. sessions we have looked at Running, see what you can remember . . .

1. Name three main muscles used in your legs to help you run:

    1. _____

    2. _____

    3. _____

2. There are five important things to remember when running. To help you remember, the beginning of each word has been written for you:

S _____

H _____

A _____

R _____

K _____

Running

S H A R K

Worksheet 3

Answers for Worksheets 2 and 3

Running

1. Name three muscles used in your legs to help you run:

- *Hamstring*
- *Quadricep*
- *Calf (Gastrocnemius)*

2. Answers to S.H.A.R.K.

S | *trides*

H | *ead-high*

A | *rms*

R | *emember to breathe*

K | *nees high*

N.B.: These answers can be copied and cut-out to use on worksheets, especially for younger children to match up with each letter on pages 114 and 115.

Football Wordsearch

Can you find these words that are important in football in the grid below?

FOOTBALL	PENALTY	GOAL KEEPER
REFEREE	LINESMAN	STRIKER
FREE-KICK	GOAL POSTS	DEFENDER
BOOTS	SHIN PADS	MIDFIELD

```
G O A L K E E P E R P L F G S D
E A D R K S P D M N O I A B F G
E C Y A N T I F U T D N G Y K K
P P G P E N A D S R T E B O U L
E F B T L E H F Y P E S F N F S
R R D K D T A S J B L M L F B L
F E S R C V E J U A N A M C O I
C E F H P I T S R E T N S J O A
L K T U D E F E N D E R R K T D
M I M J O B Y H G H N H U B S F
O C N F O O T B A L L V D F P N
W K H T N J L Z O I G D S A I W
N O N L D P N E T S H M O R T S
A Z F S H I N P A D S G E K G P
B H I P Q U Y T D T C N P J O A
S M A L A V Q O E O D G F G A K
K D I O U N S T R I K E R I L T
G R F D H I K J D U M T S N P R
J T G E F B O H O T N M T C O E
P O K N H I L S N D B W S R S F
I O N A G R E O G H R V Q O T E
D S T L D K M L P S N F L D S R
F N O F S Y V T D C H K I S E E
S P E N A L T Y N O L F G H T E
```

Football Wordsearch

Can you find these words that are important in football in the grid below?

FOOTBALL	PENALTY	GOAL KEEPER
REFEREE	LINESMAN	STRIKER
FREE-KICK	GOAL POSTS	DEFENDER
BOOTS	SHIN PADS	MIDFIELD

```
G O A L K E E P E R P L F G S D
E A D R K S P D M N O I A B F G
E C Y A N T I F U T D N G Y K K
P P G P E N A D S R T E B O U L
F F B T L E H F Y P E S F N F S
R R D K D T A S J B L M L F B L
F E S R C V E J U A N A M C O I
C E F H P I T S R E T N S J O A
L K T U D E F E N D E R R K T D
M I M J O B Y H G H N H U B S F
O C N F O O T B A L L V D F P N
W K H T N J L Z O I G D S A I W
N O N L D P N E T S H M O R T S
A Z F S H I N P A D S G E K G P
B H I P Q U Y T D T C N P J O A
S M A L A V Q O E O D G F G A K
K D I O U N S T R I K E R I L T
G R F D H I K J D U M T S N P R
J T G E F B O H O T N M T C O E
P O K N H I L S N D B W S R S F
I O N A G R E O G H R V Q O T E
D S T L D K M L P S N F L D S R
F N O F S Y V T D C H K I S E E
S P E N A L T Y N O L F G H T E
```

Worksheet 2 - **Football**

Can you label the picture?

Labels for Worksheet 2

Football

Can be cut out and glued on the worksheet.

Ball

Goal Posts

Goal Keeper

Penalty Box

Six Yard Box

Penalty Spot

Corner Flag

Referee

Assistant Referee

Kwik Cricket Wordsearch

How many of these words can you find?
Can you remember what these words mean?

STANCE	BOWLER	INNINGS
BATTING POINT	CREASE	WICKETS
PITCH	BATS	BALLS
OVER	LBW	UMPIRE

```
B A T T I N G P O I N T F G S S
E A D R K S P D M N O I A B T G
E C Y A N T I F U T D N G E K K
P P G E N A D S R T G K O U L L
E F B T L E H F Y P A C F N F S
R R O K U T A S J B I H L F B L
F G W R M V E J U W N A M C A I
C E L H P I T S R E T N C J L A
L K E U D E F K N D E R R K L D
M S R J O I Y H G H N H E B S F
O C I C P N T B A T S V A F P N
W K D R N N L Z O I G D S A I W
N O W E D I N E T S H M E R T S
A B F S O N N P F D S G E K G P
L H I P Q G Y T D T C N P J O A
S M A L A S Q O E O D G F G A K
K D I O U G S T A N C E R I P T
G R F K H I K J D U M T S N H U
J T G E F B O H O T N M T C I D
P O K N H I L S N D B W S R S P
I O N C G R O U M P I R E O R J
D S T L D K M L P S N F L D B R
F I O F S Y V T V C H K I S E E
P L O N I F O V E R L F G H T K
```

Kwik Cricket Wordsearch

How many of these words can you find?
Can you remember what these words mean?

STANCE	BOWLER	INNINGS
BATTING POINT	CREASE	WICKETS
PITCH	BATS	BALLS
OVER	LBW	UMPIRE

```
B A T T I N G P O I N T F G S S
E A D R K S P D M N O I A B T G
E C Y A N T I F U T D N G E K K
P P G P E N A D S R T G K O U L
E F B T L E H F Y P A C F N F S
R R O K U T A S J B I H L F B L
F G W R M V E J U W N A M C A I
C E L H P I T S R E T N C J L A
L K E U D E F K N D E R K L D
M S R J O I Y H G H N H E B S F
O C I C P N T B A T S V A F P N
W K D R N N L Z O I G D S A I W
N O W E D I N E T S H M E R T S
A B F S O N N P F D S G E K G P
L H I P Q G N Y T D T C N P J A
S M A L A S Q O E O D G F G A K
K D I O U G S T A N C E R I P T
G R F K H I K J D U M T S N H U
J T G E F B O H O T N M T C I D
P O K N H I L S N D B W S R S P
I O N C G R O U M P I R E O R J
D S T L D K M L P S N F L D B E
F I O F S Y V T V C H K I S E E
P L O N I F O V E R L F G H T K
```

Worksheet 2 - Kwik Cricket

Can you label the picture?

Labels for Worksheets 2

Kwik Cricket

Can be cut out and glued on the worksheet.

Bowler

Backstop

Wickets

Fielder

Crease

Batsperson

Boundary

Worksheet 3

Ways to be 'out' when batting

Can you name nine ways of being 'out' in Kwik Cricket whilst in bat?

Look at the following pictures to help you. (They can be copied and cut out as cards to match with the labels.)

1. _____

2. _____

3. _____

4. _____

5. _____

6. _____

7. _____

8. _____

9. _____

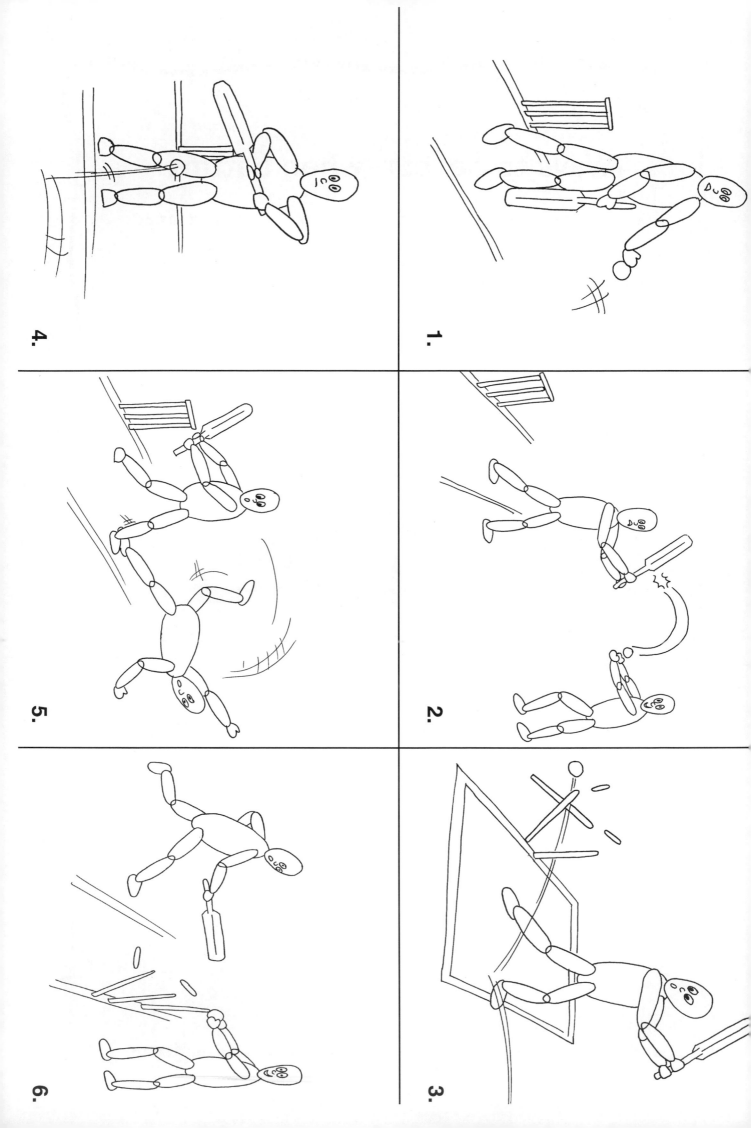

1.

2.

3.

4.

5.

6.

Bowled	Obstruction	Hit Wicket
	7.	8.
Run out	Handling	Stumped
Caught	Leg Before Wicket	Hitting the ball twice
		9.

Ways to be 'out' when batting

1. **Bowled:**

   If the batsperson misses the ball when it is bowled and the ball hits the wickets.

2. **Run Out:**

   The fielder or backstop stumps the wickets with the ball before the batsman reaches their crease.

3. **Caught:**

   If the batsperson hits the ball and it is caught by the opposing team.

4. **Obstruction:**

   If the batsperson intentionally gets in the way of any of the fielding team.

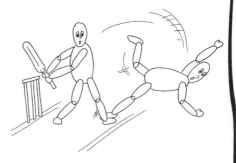

5. Handling:

If the batsperson stops the ball with their hands.

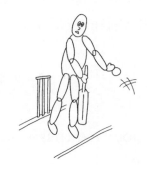

6. Leg Before Wicket:

If the batsperson stops the ball from hitting the wickets using their legs.

7. Hit wicket:

If the batsperson hits the wickets with their bat.

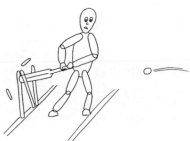

8. Stumped:

If the batsperson steps out of their crease when aiming to hit the ball, and the backstop hits the wickets with the ball.

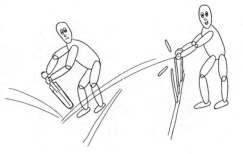

9. Hitting the ball twice:

If the batsperson hits the ball twice in one effort.

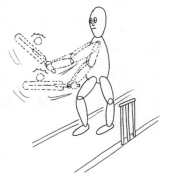

Worksheet 1

Netball Wordsearch

Can you find these words that are important in Netball in the grid below?

NETBALL	GOAL KEEPER	GOAL DEFENCE
WING ATTACK	FOOTWORK	GOAL ATTACK
WING DEFENCE	CENTRE	GOAL SHOOTER

```
F  O  O  T  W  O  R  K  A  T  B  Y  K  F  M  F
G  M  K  G  S  A  Y  T  R  G  N  L  O  G  D  L
J  O  P  F  O  B  C  K  H  B  C  E  R  H  L  O
W  T  G  D  S  A  H  I  O  B  C  I  O  T  R  K
P  T  F  H  N  O  L  L  S  T  E  U  R  S  P  G
N  R  T  U  I  N  M  S  O  Q  N  V  W  R  K  O
D  E  O  P  H  G  B  I  H  C  T  W  Y  U  M  A
C  T  T  R  S  E  B  N  O  U  R  C  D  E  M  L
G  O  A  B  F  L  L  A  B  I  E  B  Y  W  I  D
O  B  U  S  A  T  B  F  Q  W  T  S  A  I  N  E
A  T  R  E  C  L  D  E  F  G  S  L  O  N  D  F
L  G  D  E  S  V  L  R  H  D  H  R  S  G  S  E
A  P  O  U  G  S  A  V  J  I  E  D  S  A  X  N
T  W  D  W  A  E  D  W  E  P  D  C  S  T  W  C
T  C  G  E  S  A  V  T  E  W  D  X  V  T  L  E
A  R  E  S  U  X  G  E  N  G  U  L  U  A  Y  T
C  B  F  D  S  S  K  E  T  Y  U  B  R  C  W  E
K  Y  T  R  E  L  S  D  G  D  R  E  W  K  G  J
G  H  T  D  A  E  H  B  J  S  E  D  V  X  F  G
F  T  F  O  I  N  E  F  W  U  D  S  M  N  C  I
G  C  G  H  G  O  A  L  S  H  O  O  T  E  R  K
J  G  S  A  R  V  B  N  M  M  M  N  K  G  F  D
O  W  I  N  G  D  E  F  E  N  C  E  M  L  A  B
```

Netball Wordsearch

Can you find these words that are important in Netball in the grid below?

NETBALL	GOAL KEEPER	GOAL DEFENCE
WING ATTACK	FOOTWORK	GOAL ATTACK
WING DEFENCE	CENTRE	GOAL SHOOTER

```
F O O T W O R K A T B Y K F M F
G M K G S A Y T R G N L O G D L
J O P F O B C K H B C E R H L O
W T G D S A H I O B C I O T R K
P T F H N O L L S T E U R S P G
N R T U I N M S O Q N V W R K O
D E O P H G B I H C T W Y U M A
C T T R S E B N O U R C D E M L
G O A B F L L A B I E B Y W I D
O B U S A T B F Q W T S A I N E
A T R E C L D E F G S L O N D F
L G D E S V L R H D H R S G S E
A P O U G S A V J I E D S A X N
T W D W A E D W E P D C S T W C
T C G E S A V T E W D X V T L E
A R E S U X G E N G U L A Y T
C B F D S S K E T Y U B R C W E
K Y T R E L S D G D R E W K G J
G H T D A E H B J S E D V X F G
F T F O I N E F W U D S M N C I
G C G H G O A L S H O O T E R K
J G S A R V B N M M N K G F D U
O W I N G D E F E N C E M L A B
```

Worksheet 2

Netball

1. Can you label the seven positions of a netball team?

2. Using the netball court diagrams below, can you shade the area that each position is allowed to go into?

If shooting this way

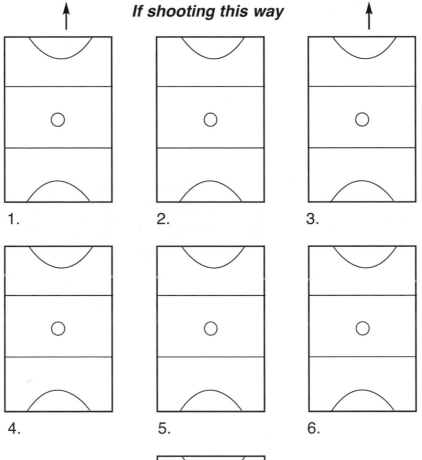

1.   2.   3.

4.   5.   6.

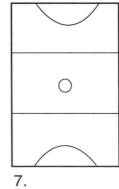

7.

Netball

1.   Can you label the seven positions of a netball team?

GK   GD   WD   C   WA   GA   GS

2.   Using the netball court diagrams below, can you shade the
      area that each position is allowed to go into?

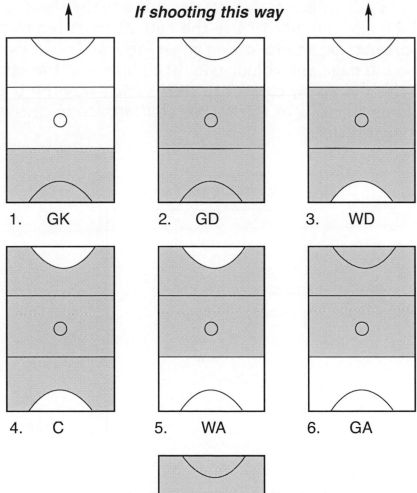

If shooting this way

1. GK   2. GD   3. WD

4. C   5. WA   6. GA

7. GS

Worksheet 3

Netball

1. How many players are there in a netball team?

2. Can you name each position? You can use the cut-outs with the initials on to help with this exercise.

3. Can you put where each player would usually stand at the beginning of the match? Use the netball court template and the cut-outs on the following pages. You will need two copies of the bib page and colour one set in blue and the other in red. Use the arrow cut-out to show which way the team would be shooting as this makes a difference on the players starting positions.

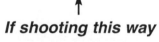

If shooting this way

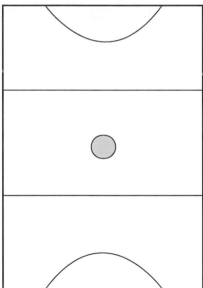

4. Can you put each player from the red team with who they would mark from the blue team? Again you can use the cutouts to help explain this.

Worksheet 3 - Answers

Netball

1. **How many players are there in a netball team?**

   7 to a team on the pitch at once.

2. **Can you name each position?**

   GA - *Goal Attack*   **GS** - *Goal Shooter*
   WA- *Wing Attack*   **C**   - *Centre*
   WD- *Wing Defence*   **GD** - *Goal Defence*
   GK - *Goal Keeper*

3. **Can you put where each player would usually stand at the beginning of the match?**

   ↑ *If shooting this way* ↑

   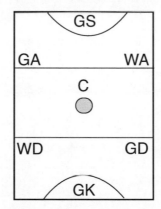

4. **Can you put each player from the red team with who they would mark from the blue team?**

RED		*BLUE*
GA - *Goal Attack*	⟶	**GD** - *Goal Defence*
GS - *Goal Shooter*	⟶	**GK** - *Goal Keeper*
WA- *Wing Attack*	⟶	**WD**- *Wing Defence*
C - *Centre*	⟶	**C** - *Centre*
WD- *Wing Defence*	⟶	**WA**- *Wing Attack*
GD - *Goal Defence*	⟶	**GA** - *Goal Attack*
GK - *Goal Keeper*	⟶	**GS** - *Goal Shooter*

Cut-outs for Netball positions

Copy twice and colour in to represent two teams.

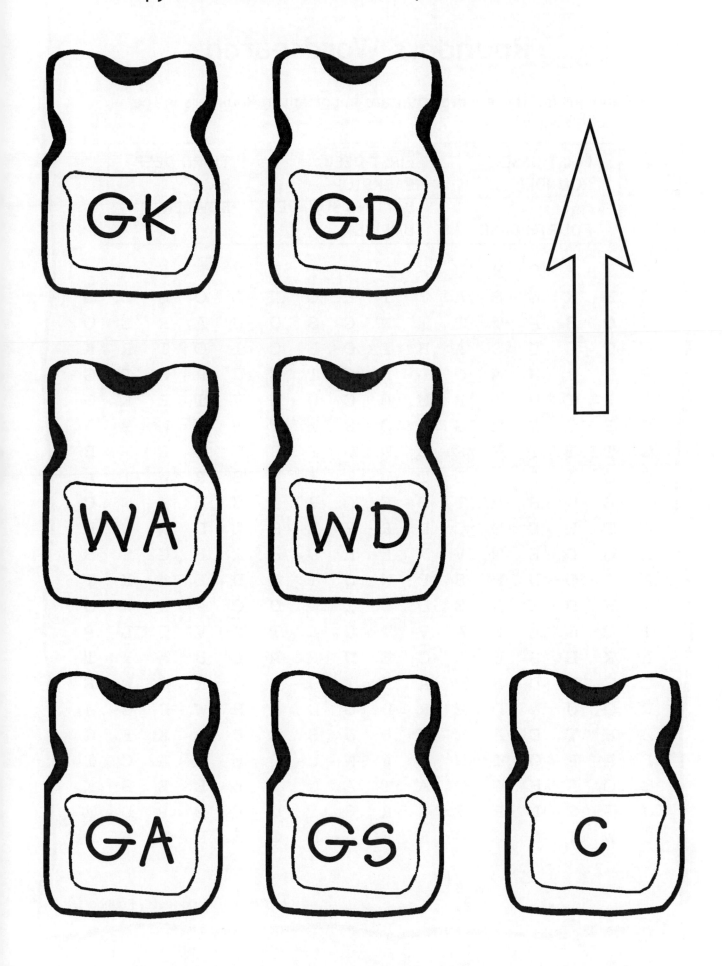

Worksheet 1

Rounders Wordsearch

Can you find these words that are important in Rounders in the grid below?

FIRST BASE	FIRST DEEP	THIRD DEEP
ROUNDER	BACKSTOP	BALL
BAT	BATTING SQUARE	BOWLER
FOURTH BASE	UMPIRE	

```
F  T  F  G  R  U  H  B  Y  T  B  Y  K  F  M  F
G  M  K  G  S  A  Y  T  R  G  N  L  O  G  D  L
J  O  B  A  T  T  I  N  G  S  Q  U  A  R  E  O
W  T  G  D  S  A  H  I  O  B  C  I  O  T  R  K
P  T  F  H  N  O  L  L  S  T  E  U  R  S  P  G
N  R  T  U  I  B  M  B  O  U  N  V  T  R  K  O
D  E  O  P  H  G  A  O  H  M  T  W  H  U  M  A
C  T  T  T  F  E  B  W  O  P  R  C  I  E  M  B
G  O  A  B  I  L  T  L  T  I  E  B  R  W  I  A
O  B  U  S  R  T  B  E  Q  R  T  S  D  I  N  C
A  T  R  E  S  C  D  R  Y  E  S  L  D  N  D  K
L  G  D  E  T  V  K  R  H  D  H  R  E  G  S  S
A  P  O  U  B  S  F  W  J  I  E  D  E  A  X  T
T  W  D  W  A  E  D  O  I  P  D  C  P  T  W  O
T  C  G  E  S  A  V  T  U  R  T  X  V  T  L  P
A  R  E  S  E  X  G  E  N  R  A  L  U  A  Y  T
C  B  F  D  S  B  A  H  T  J  T  G  R  C  W  E
R  O  U  N  D  E  R  D  G  D  S  H  W  D  G  J
B  H  T  D  A  E  H  B  J  S  E  D  B  X  F  G
F  A  F  O  I  N  E  F  W  U  D  E  M  A  C  I
G  C  L  H  G  O  A  T  A  C  I  L  E  E  S  K
J  G  S  L  R  F  I  R  S  T  D  E  E  P  D  E
O  W  I  N  G  U  E  F  J  N  C  E  M  L  A  B
```

Rounders Wordsearch

Can you find these words that are important in Rounders in the grid below?

FIRST BASE	FIRST DEEP	THIRD DEEP
ROUNDER	BACKSTOP	BALL
BAT	BATTING SQUARE	BOWLER
FOURTH BASE	UMPIRE	

```
F  T  F  G  R  U  H  B  Y  T  B  Y  K  F  M  F
G  M  K  G  S  A  Y  T  R  G  N  L  O  G  D  L
J  O  B  A  T  T  I  N  G  S  Q  U  A  R  E  O
W  T  G  D  S  A  H  I  O  B  C  I  O  T  R  K
P  T  F  H  N  O  L  L  S  T  E  U  R  S  P  G
N  R  T  U  I  B  M  B  O  U  N  V  T  R  K  O
D  E  O  P  H  G  A  O  H  M  T  W  H  U  M  A
C  T  T  T  F  E  B  W  O  P  R  C  I  E  M  B
G  O  A  B  I  L  T  L  T  I  E  B  R  W  I  A
O  B  U  S  R  T  B  E  Q  R  T  S  D  I  N  C
A  T  R  E  S  C  D  R  Y  E  S  L  D  N  D  K
L  G  D  E  T  V  K  R  H  D  H  R  E  G  S  S
A  P  O  U  B  S  F  W  J  I  E  D  E  A  X  T
T  W  D  W  A  E  D  O  I  P  D  C  P  T  W  O
T  C  G  E  S  A  V  T  U  R  T  X  V  T  L  P
A  R  E  S  E  X  G  E  N  R  A  L  U  A  Y  T
C  B  F  D  S  B  A  H  T  J  T  G  R  C  W  E
R  O  U  N  D  E  R  D  G  D  S  H  W  D  G  J
B  H  T  D  A  E  H  B  J  S  E  D  B  X  F  G
F  A  F  O  I  N  E  F  W  U  D  E  M  A  C  I
G  C  L  H  G  O  A  T  A  C  I  L  E  E  S  K
J  G  S  L  R  F  I  R  S  T  D  E  E  P  D  E
O  W  I  N  G  U  E  F  J  N  C  E  M  L  A  B
```

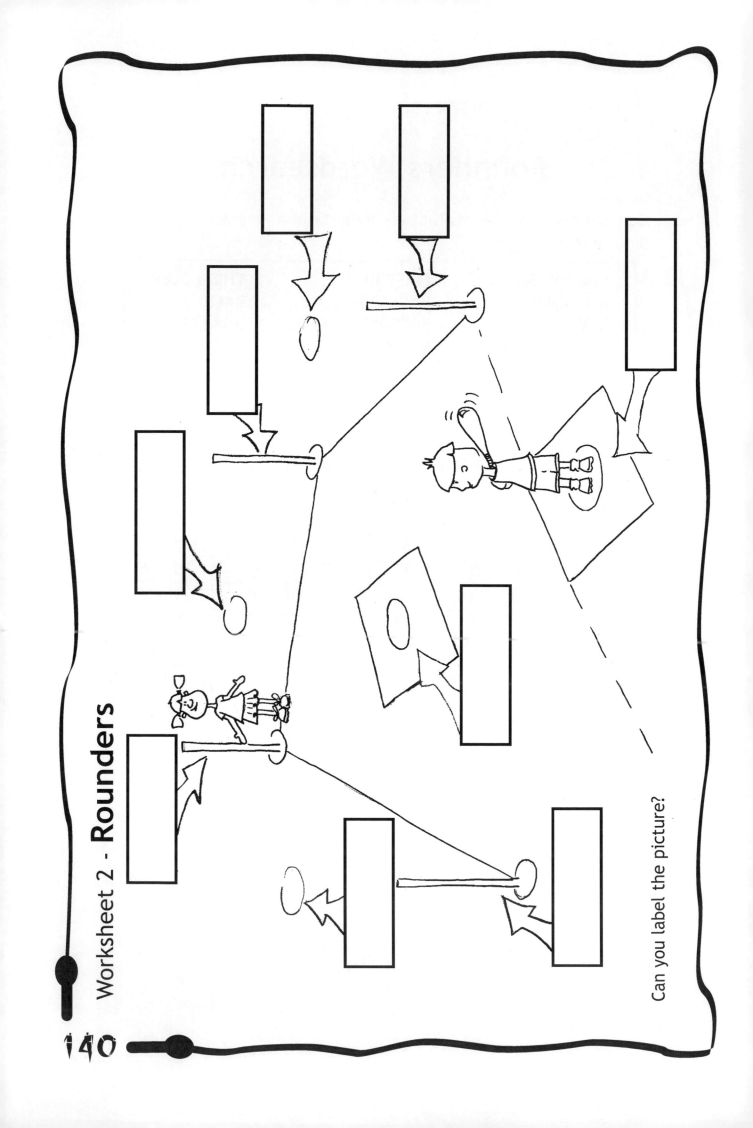

Worksheet 2 - **Rounders**

Can you label the picture?

Rounders

Can be cut out and glued on the worksheet.

Bowler

Backstop

1st Base

2nd Base

3rd Base

4th Base

1st Deep Field

2nd Deep Field

3rd Deep Field

Health and Safety Wordsearch

Can you find these words that are important in Health and Safety in the grid below?

CORRECT FOOTWEAR	NO JEWELLERY	HAIR TIDY
SAFETY	DANGERS	

```
F  T  F  G  R  U  H  B  Y  T  B  Y  K  F  M  F
G  M  K  G  S  A  Y  T  R  G  N  L  O  G  D  L
J  O  N  O  R  B  E  C  D  A  N  G  E  R  S  O
W  T  O  D  S  A  H  I  O  B  C  I  O  T  R  K
P  T  J  H  N  O  L  L  S  T  E  U  R  S  P  H
N  R  E  U  I  B  M  S  O  U  N  V  T  R  K  A
D  E  W  P  H  G  A  A  H  M  T  W  H  U  M  I
C  T  E  T  F  E  B  F  O  P  R  C  I  E  M  R
G  O  L  B  I  L  T  E  T  I  E  B  R  W  I  T
O  B  L  S  R  T  B  T  Q  R  T  S  D  I  N  I
A  T  E  E  S  C  D  Y  Y  E  S  L  D  N  D  D
L  G  R  E  T  V  K  R  H  D  H  R  E  G  S  Y
A  P  Y  U  B  S  F  W  J  I  E  D  E  A  X  T
T  W  D  W  A  E  D  O  I  P  D  C  P  T  W  O
T  C  G  E  S  A  V  T  U  R  T  X  V  T  L  P
A  R  E  S  E  X  G  E  N  R  A  L  U  A  Y  T
C  B  F  D  S  B  A  H  T  J  T  G  R  C  W  E
R  O  U  N  D  E  R  D  G  D  S  H  W  D  G  J
B  C  O  R  R  E  C  T  F  O  O  T  W  E  A  R
F  A  F  O  I  N  E  F  W  U  D  E  M  A  C  I
G  C  L  H  G  O  A  T  A  C  I  L  E  E  S  K
J  G  S  L  R  F  I  R  S  T  D  E  E  P  D  E
O  W  I  N  G  U  E  F  J  N  C  E  M  L  A  B
```

Health and Safety Wordsearch

Can you find these words that are important in Health and Safety in the grid below?

CORRECT FOOTWEAR	NO JEWELLERY	HAIR TIDY
SAFETY	DANGERS	

```
F  T  F  G  R  U  H  B  Y  T  B  Y  K  F  M  F
G  M  K  G  S  A  Y  T  R  G  N  L  O  G  D  L
J  O  N  O  R  B  E  C  D  A  N  G  E  R  S  O
W  T  O  D  S  A  H  I  O  B  C  I  O  T  R  K
P  T  J  H  N  O  L  L  S  T  E  U  R  S  P  H
N  R  E  U  I  B  M  S  O  U  N  V  T  R  K  A
D  E  W  P  H  G  A  A  H  M  T  W  H  U  M  I
C  T  E  T  F  E  B  F  O  P  R  C  I  E  M  R
G  O  L  B  I  L  T  E  T  I  E  B  R  W  I  T
O  B  L  S  R  T  B  T  Q  R  T  S  D  I  N  I
A  T  E  E  S  C  D  Y  Y  E  S  L  D  N  D  D
L  G  R  E  T  V  K  R  H  D  H  R  E  G  S  Y
A  P  Y  U  B  S  F  W  J  I  E  D  E  A  X  T
T  W  D  W  A  E  D  O  I  P  D  C  P  T  W  O
T  C  G  E  S  A  V  T  U  R  T  X  V  T  L  P
A  R  E  S  E  X  G  E  N  R  A  L  U  A  Y  T
C  B  F  D  S  B  A  H  T  J  T  G  R  C  W  E
R  O  U  N  D  E  R  D  G  D  S  H  W  D  G  J
B  C  O  R  R  E  C  T  F  O  O  T  W  E  A  R
F  A  F  O  I  N  E  F  W  U  D  E  M  A  C  I
G  C  L  H  G  O  A  T  A  C  I  L  E  E  S  K
J  G  S  L  R  F  I  R  S  T  D  E  E  P  D  E
O  W  I  N  G  U  E  F  J  N  C  E  M  L  A  B
```

Worksheet 2

Health and Safety

Can you see what is wrong in each picture? How can each danger be minimised?

1. **Danger:**

   _____

   _____

   What should be done?

   _____

   _____

   _____

2. **Danger:**

   _____

   _____

   What should be done?

   _____

   _____

   _____

3. **Danger:**

   _____

   _____

   What should be done?

   _____

   _____

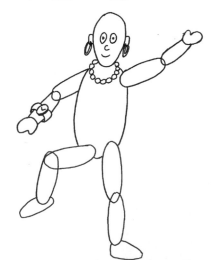

4. **Danger:**

_____

_____

What should be done?

_____

_____

_____

5. **Danger:**

_____

_____

What should be done?

_____

_____

_____

6. **Danger:**

_____

_____

What should be done?

_____

_____

_____

Health and Safety

Can you see what is wrong in each picture? How can each danger be minimised?

1. **Danger:**

   Long hair not tied back.

   What should be done?

   Tie long hair back!

2. **Danger:**

   Slippery surface.

   What should be done?

   Before an activity starts, check for spillages and slippery surfaces.

3. **Danger:**

   Jewellery.

   What should be done?

   All jewellery should be removed before exercise.

4. **Danger:**

Incorrect footwear.

What should be done?

All footwear worn must be safe
and suitable for the activity.

5. **Danger:**

Tripping over loose wires.

What should be done?

The area should be
checked for any loose wires
or objects.

6. **Danger:**

Falling from broken
equipment.

What should be done?

Check all equipment
regularly and do not use
broken equipment.

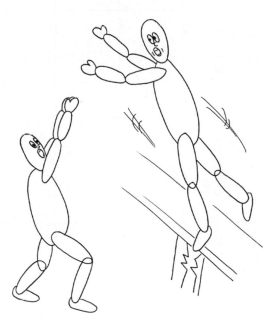

Worksheet 1 - Sports Wordsearch

Can you see any equipment three times in a row? Can you name the sport the equipment belongs to?

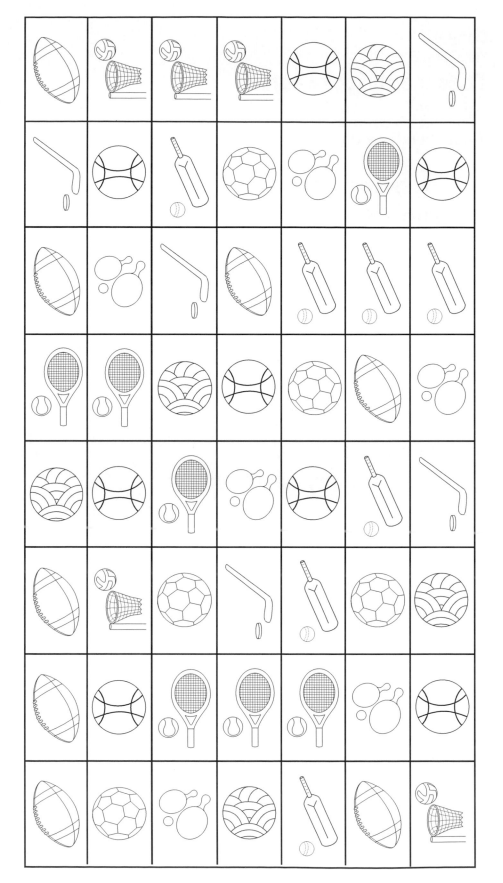

1. _____ 2. _____ 3. _____ 4. _____

Worksheet 2

Sports

Can you name the sport each picture belongs to?

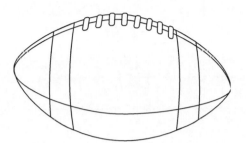

1. _____

2. _____

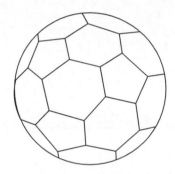

3. _____

4. _____

5. _____

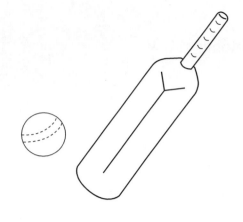

6. _____

7. _____

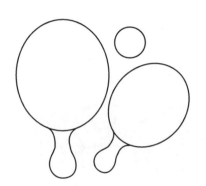

8. _____

9. _____

Sports

Can you name the sport each picture belongs to?

1. Rugby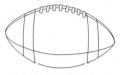

2. Basketball

3. Football

4. Volleyball

5. Tennis

6. Kwik Cricket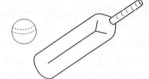

7. Netball

8. Table Tennis

9. Hockey

Worksheet 3
Sports Crossword
Use the clues to fill in all the spaces in the crossword.

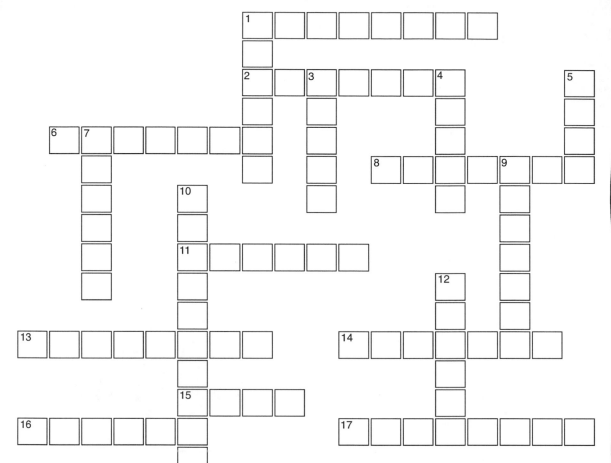

ACROSS

1. Player who stands behind the batsperson in Rounders.
2. When bowling in cricket you throw the ball at these, and when in bat you try and stop the ball from hitting these.
6. The person who is in charge of a football match, often with a whistle and sometimes wears a black shirt and black shorts.
8. In Rounders if you are not in the batting team you are a . . . .   .
11. In Football there are 3 main positions Defence, Midfield and . . . . .   .
13. The position David Beckham plays and involves a lot of running in Football.
14. In Rounders if you hit the ball and run around all of the posts in one go you score a . . . . .
15. In Netball, Chest, Bounce and Shoulder are all types of . . . .
16. The name for a referee of a netball match.
17. If you get fouled in Football you can be awarded a . . . . .

DOWN

1. The person who throws the ball to the person in bat when playing Rounders or Cricket.
3. The area a Netball match is played on: A Netball . . . . .
4. The number of players in a Netball team.
5. The number of posts to run around in Rounders.
7. The number of players in a Football team (Not including Substitutes).
9. The player who would mark Goal Attack in netball is Goal . . . . .
10. The person who defends the goal in Football and who is the only player allowed to use their hands.
12. In Netball, the player who is allowed on the whole court except in the semi-circles.

Sports Crossword

Use the clues to fill in all the spaces in the crossword.

```
                    ¹B  A  C  K  S  T  O  P
                     O
                    ²W  I  ³C  K  E  T  ⁴S              ⁵F
                     L      O          E               O
        ⁶R  ⁷E  F  E  R  E  E      O          V               U
            L          R      U      ⁸F  I  E  L  ⁹D  E  R
            E      ¹⁰G          T          N      E
            V          O                          F
            E      ¹¹A  T  T  A  C  K              E
            N          L              ¹²C          N
                       K               E          C
        ¹³M  I  D  F  I  E  L  D      ¹⁴R  O  U  N  D  E  R
                       E               T
                    ¹⁵P  A  S  S       R
        ¹⁶U  M  P  I  R  E          ¹⁷F  R  E  E  K  I  C  K
                       R
```

ACROSS

1. Player who stands behind the batsperson in Rounders.
2. When bowling in cricket you throw the ball at these, and when in bat you try and stop the ball from hitting these.
6. The person who is in charge of a football match, often with a whistle and sometimes wears a black shirt and black shorts.
8. In Rounders if you are not in the batting team you are a . . . .   .
11. In Football there are 3 main positions Defence, Midfield and . . . . .   .
13. The position David Beckham plays and involves a lot of running in Football.
14. In Rounders if you hit the ball and run around all of the posts in one go you score a . . . . .
15. In Netball, Chest, Bounce and Shoulder are all types of . . . .
16. The name for a referee of a netball match.
17. If you get fouled in Football you can be awarded a . . . . .

DOWN

1. The person who throws the ball to the person in bat when playing Rounders or Cricket.
3. The area a Netball match is played on: A Netball . . . . .
4. The number of players in a Netball team.
5. The number of posts to run around in Rounders.
7. The number of players in a Football team (Not including Substitutes).
9. The player who would mark Goal Attack in netball is Goal . . . . .
10. The person who defends the goal in football and who is the only player allowed to use their hands.
12. In Netball, the player who is allowed on the whole court except in the semi-circles.

Worksheet 4

Sports Quiz Ideas

1) **What shirt number did David Beckham usually wear when he played for England?**
   A. 7
   B. 8
   C. 9
   D. 6

2) **What year did England men's football team last win the World Cup?**
   A. 1976
   B. 1966
   C. 1996

3) **In what sport do you associate the Ryder Cup?**
   A. Tennis
   B. Golf
   C. Horse racing

4) **What sport has an annual competition each year at Wimbledon?**
   A. Golf
   B. Tennis
   C. Netball

5) **What football team plays their home football games at White Hart Lane?**
   A. Tottenham Hotspur
   B. Aston Villa
   C. Chelsea

6) **In what sport would you demonstrate the Butterfly stroke?**
   A. Tennis
   B. Swimming
   C. Football

7) **If I had just scored a 'TRY' what sport would I be playing in?**
   A. Tennis
   B. Hockey
   C. Rugby

References

❑   Wesson, K. Wiggins, N. Thompson, G. Hartigan, S. (1998).
    Sport & PE, London. Hodder & Stoughton.

❑   www.qcq.org.uk

❑   http://www.fis.egreen.wednet.edu/classrooms/pe/YPE.html

❑   http://www.vis.ac.at/primary/departments/physical_education

Appendices

Running Times

Distances based on one length of netball court, approx. 90m.
For weeks 2 and 4. Do two runs per week and take best time.

| Name | Week 2 | | Week 4 | | Improvement Yes/No |
	Sprint 1	Sprint 2	Sprint 1	Sprint 2	

Sports Quiz Answer Sheet

Team Name: _____

Question Number	Round 1	Round 2	Round 3	Round 4	Round 5